My Classic Radio Interviews With The Stars

Also by Award Winning
Actor/Award Winning Author/
Celebrity Radio Talk Show Host

Michael Dante

Michael Dante – From Hollywood to Michael Dante Way
Autobiography (2014)
Received the 'Ella Dickey Literacy Award' in 2018

Winterhawk's Land – A Novella (2017)
Sequel story to the 1975 film *Winterhawk* with Michael Dante starring in the title role in the film as Blackfoot Chief Winterhawk.

Six Rode Home – A Novella (2018)
Civil War yarn. Six horse soldiers return home to…what?

My Classic Radio Interviews With The Stars

Volume One

By Michael Dante

Co-Authored by Mary Jane Dante

Edited by Marshall Terrill

BearM anor Media

2021

My Classic Radio Interviews With the Stars, Volume 1

© 2021 Michael Dante

All rights reserved.

For information, address:

BearManor Media
1317 Edgewater Dr #110
Orlando FL 32804
bearmanormedia.com

Cover Design by Mary Jane Dante

Typesetting and layout by John Teehan

Published in the USA by BearManor Media

ISBN—978-1-62933-760-9

Dedication Page

This book is dedicated to all my legendary celebrity friends, who contributed their time and creative talent as guests on my radio show. Without them, this book couldn't have been written.

To my wife, Mary Jane, who recorded the interviews with her technical skill and co-wrote this book with me as 'Team Dante.'

To Marshall Terrill, who edited this book with his expertise and knowledge of literary excellence.

Always to God, for gifting me with all the talent it takes to be creative and inventive and to Mom and Dad who gave me incentive by example.

I am eternally grateful to be able to share my incomparable, timeless and entertaining classic radio interviews with the stars, from the Golden Age of Hollywood.

Table of Contents

Foreword xi

Introduction 1

1   Anna Maria Alberghetti 3
2   Kaye Ballard 6
3   Johnny Bench 9
4   Milton Berle 12
5   Yogi Berra 15
6   Pat Boone 18
7   Eric Braeden 21
8   Dick Butkus 24
9   Rory Calhoun 27
10 Glen Campbell 30
11 Rosie Casals 33
12 Norm Crosby 36
13 Tony Curtis 40
14 Beryl Davis 43
15 Ann Meyers Drysdale 46
16 James Farentino 49
17 Rhonda Fleming 52
18 Robert Forster 55

19	Connie Francis	58
20	Shecky Greene	61
21	Anne Jeffreys	64
22	Lainie Kazan	67
23	Howard Keel	70
24	Harmon Killebrew	73
25	Ralph Kiner	77
26	Morgana King	80
27	Frankie Laine	83
28	Tommy Lasorda	86
29	Rod Laver	90
30	Carol Lawrence	93
31	Robert Loggia	96
32	Trini López III	99
33	Maurice Lucas	102
34	Carol Lynley	105
35	James MacArthur	108
36	Gavin & Patti MacLeod	112
37	Virginia Mayo	115
38	Barbara McNair	118
39	Gerald McRaney	122
40	Robert Morse	125
41	Don Murray	128
42	Julie Newmar	131
43	Charlie Pasarell	134

44	Stephanie Powers	137
45	Debbie Reynolds	140
46	Andy Robustelli	144
47	Keely Smith	147
48	Elke Sommer	150
49	Rod Steiger	153
50	Connie Stevens	156
51	George Takei	159
52	Constance Towers	163
53	Jerry Vale	166
54	Mamie Van Doren	169
55	Ken Venturi	172
56	Clint Walker	176
57	Joseph Wambaugh	179
58	Dawn Wells	182
59	Jerry West	186
60	Jonathan Winters	189

The career details included about each celebrity is only up to the date of our interview. What they accomplished afterward is not included in their chapter. All celebrity quotes are in their own words and the tense reflects the passages as they were written at the time.

Foreword
by Gavin MacLeod

I WOULD LIKE TO INTRODUCE YOU, the reader and eventually the listener, to a most unique and special book. In fact, it's about a one-of-a-kind radio interview show created, hosted and co-produced by my friend, award-winning actor and award-winning author, Michael Dante. The radio shows were recorded and co-produced by his talented, creative and technically savvy wife, Mary Jane Dante. Today, they are known as 'Team Dante.'

Michael and Mary Jane Dante are a team in more ways than one. They met in 1990 and married in 1992. It was baseball that initially introduced them, but their backgrounds in the film industry is what brought them together as a team.

Michael worked in front of the camera as a handsome, talented and charismatic actor after a shoulder injury shortened his professional baseball career. He was on a two-week leave of absence from baseball when Tommy Dorsey, the famous bandleader, saw him in a play at the University of Miami. He told Dante if his shoulder didn't come around, he wanted to set up a screen test for him at MGM Studios. Well, the shoulder didn't come around. But Michael took that screen test and had been under contract to three major studios, MGM, Warner Bros. and 20th Century Fox where he co-starred, starred and guest starred in approximately 30 films and 150 television shows.

Michael has received many prestigious awards in and out of Hollywood, is accomplished as a radio show host, and in 2018 became a published, award-winning author. His autobiography *Michael Dante-From Hollywood to Michael Dante Way*, about his journey through the Golden Years of Hollywood, is a spectacular read.

Michael followed that endeavor with two novellas, *Winterhawk's Land*, the sequel to the film, *Winterhawk*, in which he played the title role, and *Six Rode Home*, a Civil War yarn dedicated to all the men and women who have served our country, in all wars. Knowing and working with so many of his famous peers, he was ready to write this book about his radio show years.

Mary Jane came from a baseball family. Her father, Mark Scott, was the host and one of the originators of the original *Home Run Derby*. She was at the Southern California Sports Broadcasters Luncheon in Los Angeles in 1990, a gathering her dad and Tom Harmon originated in the 1950s. Michael was one of the guest speakers that day and the two met, fell madly in love, and have been married for over 25 years. Mary Jane was there on her lunch break from the Walt Disney Studios, where she worked as a film editor.

She spent 25 years behind the scenes as a film technician and editor at Universal Studios, Paramount Studios and Disney Studios and had learned much about the technical aspect of filmmaking. Mary Jane, along with Disney's trailer department's editing team, created 250 theatrical trailers. Her trailer for the film *Sister Act* starring Whoopi Goldberg, helped Disney Studios sell the film. It was a huge success, grossing more than $230 million worldwide. She also enjoyed recording voiceovers for television and radio commercials for many years in Palm Springs, California.

While on vacation in Stamford, Connecticut (Michael's hometown where he has a street named after him, Michael Dante Way) in the early 1990s, Michael and Mary Jane were driving to a friend's home on a beautiful summer's day in the northeast. At that time, Michael hosted a radio show in the Palm Springs, California area, where he and Mary Jane lived. The owner of the station signed Michael for 13 weeks as a host, loved what he did and wanted him to sign another 13-week contract. It was a great compliment to Michael's talents, but that's when he realized he'd be better off doing his own show.

With all the celebrities Michael knew, it wouldn't be difficult at all. Michael was confident and shared his idea with Mary Jane on that drive and when they returned home, they began to work on their project, *The Michael Dante Classic Celebrity Talk Show*.

Their formula for success came as Michael knew so many stars from the world of entertainment and sports. He was literally able to just pick up the phone, call them at home and ask if and when they were available for a recorded interview. We're talking over 250 plus celebrities, and everyone said yes! That's a pretty good record and a testament to the friendship, respect and trust that all of the great stars had for Michael. The celebrity guests loved doing the show and that sentiment is reflected in every interview in this book. Each one sounds more like a fireside chat rather than just an interview. I know because my wife Patti and I had the most wonderful interview with Michael.

Using her technical skills and background in film editing, Mary Jane recorded the interviews on her Marantz recorder, mixing board and microphones. They worked together and co-produced each show, thriving for perfection, and with perfect timing. Michael's favorite line, "Timing's not important, it's everything!" These interviews prove that point perfectly. They also had to abide by the radio station's clock, making room for sponsor's commercials in each show. It was so well done that the radio shows continued to be broadcast every week for 12 years. It was far reaching and very well-received.

Hence, Michael and Mary Jane are professionally and affectionately known as 'Team Dante.'

Now it's time to read the stories, see the photos, and listen to the interviews through (not *on*) Michael's web site at **www.michaeldanteway.com**.

And as my friend, Michael Dante would say, "I know, I just know you're gonna love it!"

Your friend, wishing you much success,
The 'Love Boat' Captain, Actor – Gavin MacLeod

Introduction
by Michael Dante

IN THE EARLY 1990S, I was interviewed on a Palm Springs, California radio station. I spoke honestly and earnestly about my life and career in sports and acting. After the interview, I was asked by the general manager if I would be interested in hosting a talk show at the radio station. I accepted by signing a 13-week contract to host a weekly one-hour celebrity talk show. He was aware that throughout my career as a professional baseball player and actor, I became friends and worked with many of the top stars from the world of entertainment and sports.

After a successful 13-week run, he asked me to stay on, but I decided to create my own radio show, *The Michael Dante Classic Celebrity Talk Show*. The rest is recorded history; history that you can relive through 200 stellar interviews I hosted from 1994 to 2008, with legendary personalities from the Golden Years of Hollywood and the wonderful world of sports. This book was written to share highlights about their personal career stories and to interest the reader to learn more about the stars through my one hour interviews.

People in the Palm Springs area and the Coachella Valley remember these awesome interviews with great enthusiasm because of the exclusive position I was in. I was able to bring classic actors, actresses, entertainers and sports figures to the airwaves, and it was like listening to friends having a fireside chat. My wife, Mary Jane recorded the shows as we worked together to produce something very special and to be able to share these classic interviews and one-of-a-kind, timeless recordings with you.

I know, I just know you're gonna love it!

Anna Maria Alberghetti
Entertainer
Interviewed: 1996

I MET THE MULTI-TALENTED PERFORMER Anna Maria Alberghetti in the late 1950s. That's when my friend, actor and restauranteur, Nicky Blair, invited me to go with him to meet Anna and her family. Their lovely home was located near the Sunset Strip in Hollywood, California, around the corner from the famous Schwab's Drugstore. Many actors, actresses and entertainers were discovered there.

The moment I met Anna and her parents, I felt like I was at home with my own family. Opera music flowed softly throughout their home with a beautiful grand piano placed perfectly in the living room. Whenever I drove past Anna's house, I could hear her rehearsing with the accompaniment of her mom on the piano. Our paths didn't cross very often in Hollywood, and it wasn't until many years later when I saw her again, and asked if she would be a guest on my radio show. She could not have been nicer in accepting my invitation.

Anna, as she is called by her friends, was born in Pesaro, Italy. The daughter of a concert master father and a pianist mother, she began singing at the age of six. "I cannot remember a time when music was not a part of my life," Anna recalled. "My father sang with a number of famous opera companies, including at La Scala and he was concertmaster for the Rome Opera Company." Her father was also her only vocal instructor.

After World War II, Anna's parents brought her to America, where she debuted at Carnegie Hall. A *New York Times* critic was amazed by her extraordinary talents.

The *Times* review glowed about Anna's talent, "Some of the purest, loveliest sounds that ever been heard." Anna continued to be successful with the New York Philharmonic and other distinguished symphonies, as a soloist with some of the most revered orchestras in the country.

Ed Sullivan introduced Anna Maria Alberghetti to television audiences and her performance in the Broadway classic *Carnival* won her a Tony Award as Best Actress in

Anna Maria Alberghetti

a Musical. She has given unforgettable performances in *West Side Story, Sound of Music, Cabaret, Camelot, Fannie, Most Happy Fella, The Boyfriend, Student Prince* and *Side-by-Side by Sondheim*. Her recording career included contracts with Capitol Records, Columbia Records, Mercury Records and MGM Records.

Alberghetti's feature films include *The Medium, Here Comes the Groom, The Stars Are Singing, 10,000 Bedrooms, The Last Command,* and *Cinderella*. She starred with some of Hollywood's favorite leading men such as Dean Martin, Bing Crosby, Metropolitan Opera great Lawrence Melchior and Jerry Lewis.

She performed with the California Glendale Symphony at the Los Angeles Music Center, then in a series of concerts in Illinois, Florida and Ohio. She later teamed with her good friend, John Raitt, for an enchanted evening of Broadway music that toured across the country, and was loved and appreciated by all who attended.

Alberghetti has two daughters from her marriage to director/producer Claudio Guzman. "When you've been fortunate enough to have a career as a child, there are great advantages and great responsibilities. I accomplished so many things during the early days of my career that I never did feel the sacrifice in being home with my children. Rather, there was joy." About her career, Anna said, "Some people have just attended a concert, others were touched by a lecture, or one of my films has entertained them. It's satisfying and special to be familiar to so many people."

It was talent like Anna's that made Hollywood so special during its Golden Years.

2

Kaye Ballard
Entertainer
Interviewed: 1995

I DON'T KNOW WHERE THE TIME has gone, but it seems just like yesterday that I met gifted Kaye Ballard at Rita and Jerry Vale's dinner party at their home in Beverly Hills, California. Kaye was so funny and we enjoyed her humor. I saw her a few times after that evening around Hollywood and was happy to learn we both became residents of Rancho Mirage, California, several years later. My wife Mary Jane and I spotted Kaye many times at social events in the Palm Springs area. She was always the same, warm and friendly with that great sense of humor.

Kaye Ballard launched her career as a comic-tuba player with the Spike Jones Band, followed by vaudeville tours with Vaughn Monroe and Stan Kenton. That led to Broadway in leading roles with Phil Silvers in *Top Banana* and *Three to Make Ready* with Ray Bolger which led to her stardom. Several Broadway plays and musicals followed such as *The Golden Apple, Carnival, Molly, The Beast in Me, Wonderful Town, The Pirates of Penzance,* to name a few. In addition, her critically acclaimed one-woman shows, *Kaye Ballard Working 42nd St. At Last* and *Hey Mamma, Kaye Ballard,* both received The Drama Desk and Outer Critics Circle Award nominations. Kaye remarked, "What's fascinating for me, is to realize I'm a very square singer. I'm a Broadway singer. I sing a melody. And to work with someone you love is great. David Merrick was one of the all-time great producers." Kaye made her motion picture debut in the Gower Champion Musical, *The Girl Most Likely.* Ballard smiled, "As corny as it sounds, Gower was my champion. I worked with Gower a lot and I adored Gower. And Gower used to say to people 'Don't judge Kaye by a rehearsal.' In rehearsal, I don't really give what I'm gonna give during the show."

Kaye followed with several other roles, working with Shelley Winters, Jerry Lewis, Patrick Swayze, Robbie Benson and Jon Voight. She also starred in *Crazy Words, Crazy Tunes* and shared that, "It was in the Convention Center. It was a commercial concept but I think it was in the wrong place. I felt so bad that they didn't do better than they should,

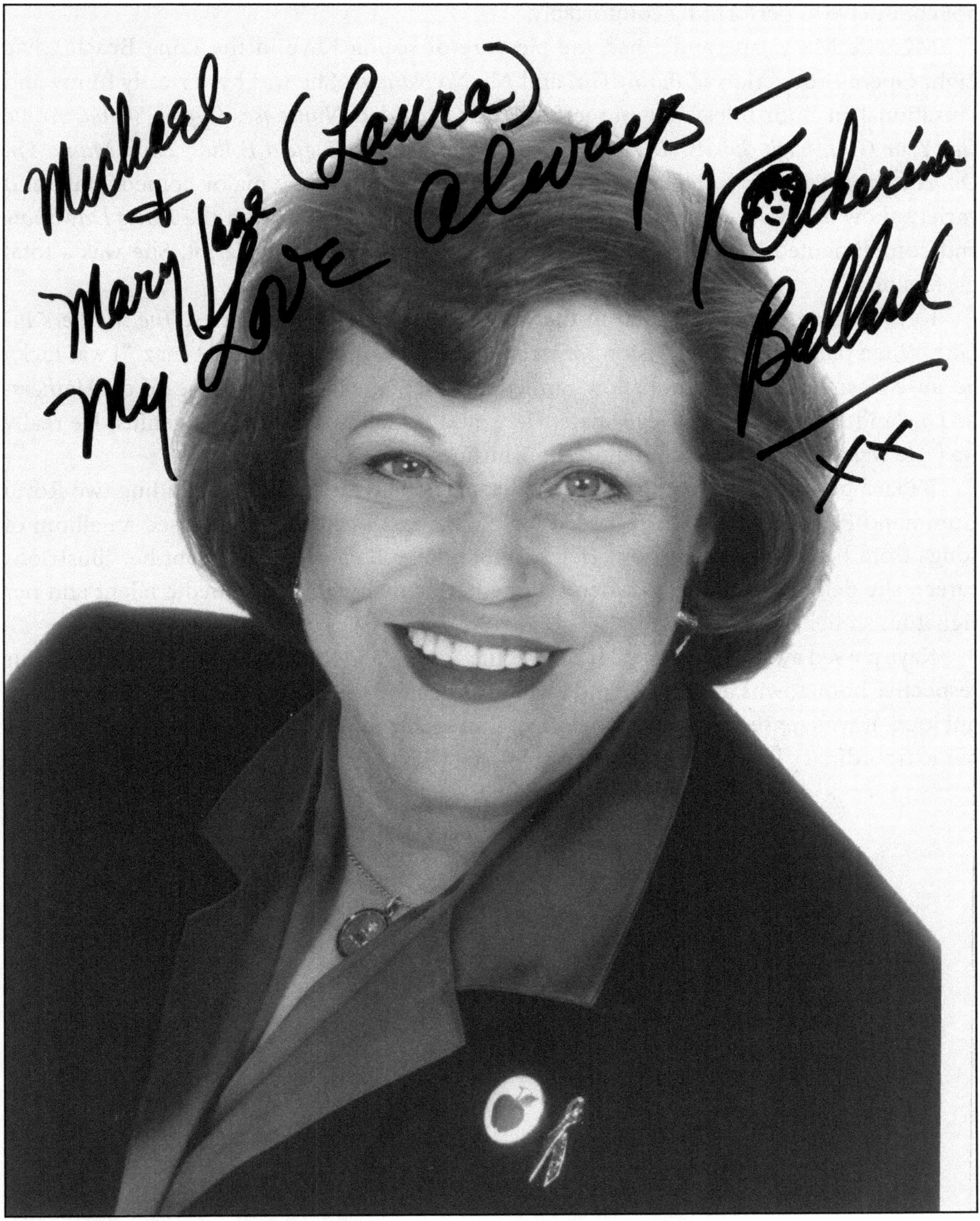
Michael
+
Mary Jane (Laura)
My Love always —
Katherina
Ballard
xx

because it's not a theater, it's an assembly hall. They didn't have the proper lighting. It's just not conducive to performing comfortably."

My wife Mary Jane and I had the pleasure of seeing Kaye in the Long Beach Civic Light Opera Production of *Funny Girl* and *No, No Nanette*. She was hysterically funny and sensational in both roles. Her numerous tours included *Nunsense, Gypsy, Sheba, Annie Get Your Gun, High Spirits, The Odd Couple, Minis Boys, Ziegfeld Follies, Look Mama I'm Dancing and Four Girls,* to name a few. She appeared on every major comedy, talk and variety show and was a regular on the Perry Como Show. She was on the *Doris Day Show* and complimented her work ethic. "Doris Day, I worked with her a lot. She was a total professional."

Kaye teamed with Eve Arden in the very successful television series, *The Mothers In-Law.* When talking about television Kaye remembered working for Desi Arnaz. "I was lucky because Desi Arnaz would not allow canned laughter. The laughter you heard on *Mothers-In-Law* and *I Love Lucy* was legitimate. He would not allow it. He was a genius. He really was. He was the most tasteful man in show business."

Ballard performed abroad in every media, particularly in London, including two Royal Command Performances. She recorded for EMI/Angel Records and released an album of songs from her one-woman show, *Hey Mamma, Kaye Ballard*. Throughout her illustrious career, she delighted audiences wherever she performed with her comedic talent and her signature smile.

Kaye passed away on January 21, 2019 at the age of 93 in Rancho Mirage, California, our respective hometowns. Mary Jane and I will miss her and the many times she made us laugh out loud. Kaye's sense of humor with perfect timing, her smile and contagious laughter, plus her extraordinary love for animals. She is missed by all.

Johnny Bench
Major League Baseball – Hall of Fame
Interviewed: 2008

I MET JOHNNY BENCH FOR THE FIRST TIME when I took Jonathan Winters to the Cincinnati Reds locker room to meet his favorite team and to entertain them before the start of a three-game series with the Los Angeles Dodgers. Johnny thoroughly enjoyed Jonathan's routine between two disgruntled ballplayers, yelling at each other over the loud sound of each other's boombox radios. It was hysterically funny.

The next time I saw him was at the Annual Frank Sinatra Invitational in Palm Springs, California. Johnny lived in the same area, surrounded by beautiful golf courses and was one of the better players on the celebrity golf circuit. One of his ambitions when he qualified, was to play on the Senior Professional Golf Tour which comprised of players fifty years of age and over. Johnny said during our radio interview, about getting old, "A golfer friend told me that growing old is mandatory, growing up is optional."

Johnny was born in Oklahoma City, Oklahoma on December 7, 1947, and twenty years later he was catching for the Cincinnati Reds in the National League. John shared that, "The Reds drafted me and I had a chance to play on one of the greatest teams in history." In 1968 he was unanimously voted Rookie of the Year. His career expanded to seventeen years when he decided to hang up his spikes. We talked about his manager, the legendary Sparky Anderson. "When you have somebody in your life that you can bounce things off of and you can respect and feel as a friend, a mentor and a father, you're a pretty lucky person," said Bench.

By that time, he had hit more home runs than any other catcher in the history of the game at 389, knocking in 1,376 runs with a lifetime batting average of 267. Johnny played in four World Series, was voted The Most Valuable Player in the National League in 1970 and 1971 and was inducted into The Baseball Hall of Fame in 1989. Arguably, he is the greatest catcher of all time.

Johnny described his youth playing baseball for our listeners, "On our little league teams and high school teams, I hardly ever caught. But everybody knew I was a catcher, but I didn't catch. I didn't get to catch until I was 17 years old. I pitched and played the bases, but didn't catch."

Bench liked radio and after his playing days, he went to work for CBS as an analyst for 10 years. My friend Norman Baer, a producer of CBS major-league baseball radio, said Johnny was the best color man and analyst who ever worked for him. He continued his radio career doing many commercials and then entered the television world doing many commercials on camera. To this day he is in demand doing television commercials, selling several popular healthcare products. John's book, *Catch Every Ball – How to Handle Life's Pitches,* is something he is also very proud of accomplishing.

One of his favorite pastimes is listening to country music and singing country songs. I heard him sing on many occasions and he had that good country accent with a deep voice that reminded me of the older country and western singers.

I've known Johnny for a long time and I see him from time to time in the Palm Springs area at what's left of the celebrity golf circuit. We always share a few laughs when we meet. His sense of humor has never left him. When I hear his name or think about knowing Johnny Bench, I say to myself, "Michael, in your lifetime you were pals with one of the greatest catchers of all time."

He was blessed with talent and I am blessed with his friendship.

Milton Berle
Entertainer
Interviewed: 1994

I MET ENTERTAINER, STAR OF THEATER, vaudeville, films, television, radio and nightclubs, Mr. Milton Berle, at the Friars Club in Beverly Hills, California. Jerry Vale and I were there having lunch and he knew and worked with Milton on numerous occasions, so we went over to his booth to say hello. He had his own booth at the club, where he had lunch on a daily basis and did business with his writers, producers, directors and agents. Milton and two of his writers were there, and we all had an immediate connection. The table was full of energy and laughter from the moment we arrived and to the moment we left.

I saw Berle several times at Café Roma Restaurant in Beverly Hills and he greeted me warmly every time. I told him about my radio show and asked if he would like to do an interview with me. He responded very nicely, saying, "Call me at the Friars Club and we'll set a date to do it at lunch hour at the club." About a week later, I had the pleasure of interviewing Mr. Television, Mr. Entertainment and Mr. Show Business, but to me he will always be Uncle Miltie. Every time I saw him after our interview, I called him Uncle Miltie, and he liked that.

Milton Berle, in every aspect of show business, for over 80 years, was one of the all-time greats of the entertainment world. He was born in Harlem, New York and started in show business at the age of five. Yes, it was true that he was the Buster Brown boy. "I was the Buster Brown boy, and I was the Buster Brown shoes. I was a boy model; I was in ads and papers with a prince valiant haircut. Charlie Chaplin saw me in one of those ads and I went to California in 1913."

Berle was also the baby that was tossed from a speeding train in the *Perils of Pauline*, and the baby that Marie Dressler clutched to her heart in, *Tillie's Punctured Romance*. Milton told us about his mom, who was always there.

"Mother was always traveling with me, laughing it up from the audience. If there was a stage mother, it was my mother, Sarah. She made Gypsy Rose Lee's mother look like

Mary Poppins." Milton had a thoughtful moment and shared, "Family values are very, very important, especially family value entertainment."

He made vaudeville history as the youngest master of ceremonies at B.F. Keith's Palace Theater. "If you want to go back to vaudeville, that's way before the nightclubs. I appeared in vaudeville from 1916 until I went into nightclubs." It led him to starring engagements in Earl Carol's *Vanities*. "I sang the song, "I Got a Right to Sing the Blues" and it became a hit."

He also starred in George Abbott's *See My Lawyer*, George White's *Scandals* and the 1935 version of the *Ziegfeld Follies*. Milton's café appearances were the ultimate at Billy Rose's Casino de Paris, Broadway's International Casino and New York's Carnival. On radio, he distinguished himself with *The Gillette Community Sing, Stop Me If You Heard This One, Can You Top This, Let Yourself Go*, and the incredible list goes on.

In 1948, he became televisions first giant, so to speak, when he launched the *Texaco Star Theater* for NBC. Milton added, "That was back in 1948 when I first went on, June 13, 1948, for the Texaco Star Theater and being the first one to take a shot at television. And Joe E. Lewis, who introduced me to the audience at the Copacabana at the height of my popularity on the Texaco Show, in the '50s." Milton directed, produced and wrote with a staff of writers for every show he did, including *The Berle Buick Show, Jackpot Bowling, Kraft Music Hall, The Milton Berle Show* and many outstanding television specials.

Milton won four Emmy Awards and was nominated for best dramatic performance in *Doyle Against the House*. He was the first star to host a telethon in 1949, for the Damon Runyon Cancer Fund. Wherever there was a good deed, Milton was always there.

He was inducted into The Television Hall of Fame and received a special plaque awarded him from the Academy of Television Arts and Sciences, that he would now be known as 'Mr. Television.'

"At age seventeen, I got a call from the *Guinness Book of Records*. They asked me the question, how many shows or benefits did you do? Over 44,000! Since nine years old, during WWI, 1917, I started working with Irving Berlin and travelled with him doing camp shows."

Berle was under contract to 20th Century Fox for four years and made twenty pictures there, such as *Tall, Dark and Handsome, Sun Valley Serenade, Always Leave Them Laughing, The Loved One, Gentleman at Heart, It's A Mad, Mad, Mad, Mad World, The Happening*, and his terrific performance that always stands out in my mind, his dramatic work in *The Oscar*. He was sensational. 'The King of Comedy' aka Milton Berle, wrote and published over four hundred songs and authored several books. He was the only actor to appear on the covers of *Time* and *Newsweek* magazines in the same week. He said, "It was quite a hectic career and it wasn't easy; it wasn't easy. Lotta hard work. I enjoyed it."

I'll always remember the fashion show that Milton's wife, Lorna and I modeled in for a celebrity charity benefit in Beverly Hills, California. Stella Stevens was one of the models, too. Milton attended and performed for the audience and made us all laugh, as usual. He was hysterically funny. Those are very special and fond memories of happy days gone by. This giant in the entertainment industry left us in 2002 at age 93.

As Milton Berle would say, with tongue-in-cheek humor, "We had a lotta laugh. Drumbeat…1, 2, 3."

Yes, we sure did, up until the day he left us.

Yogi Berra
Major League Baseball – Hall of Fame
Interviewed: 1995

I MET LAWRENCE PETER 'YOGI' BERRA and his wife Carmen many years ago at the Annual Frank Sinatra Invitational. As the years went by, we played a few times prior to the beginning of the Sinatra Golf Classic in preparation, as a warm up round before the tournament started.

Yogi was a joy to be with. He had a humble, down-to-earth personality. He loved to play golf but unfortunately, he never had the time to properly devote himself to the game. Residing in New Jersey didn't give him the opportunity to play golf that much, because after the baseball season was over, the weather turned cold and snowy. Throughout the years, Mary Jane and I called Yogi and Carmen to say hello. They were always so gracious and happy to hear from us, and even said they enjoyed seeing me on television in different shows.

Yogi Berra enjoyed an outstanding career. He played seventeen years in the New York Yankees organization. He hit 358 home runs, had a lifetime batting average of 285 and played in fourteen World Series. Yogi was voted three times the American League's Most Valuable Player in 1951 and in consecutive years 1954 and 1955. He holds the major league record for playing in the most World Series games at 75, most at bats at 259, most hits at 71 and most doubles at 10. He was second in runs batted in with 39, third in home runs with 12 and walked 32 times.

Yogi had the reputation of being a bad ball hitter. That's ironic because one of the most interesting and phenomenal statistics about Yogi Berra occurred in 1950, when he came to the plate 597 times, hit 28 home runs, had 124 runs batted in and only struck out 12 times. Now that's remarkable!

Yogi also managed two pennant winning teams in both the American and National Leagues; the New York Yankees in 1964 and the New York Mets in 1973. He managed for

a total of seven years. He was inducted into The Baseball Hall of Fame in 1972. Yogi Berra was undoubtably one of the most popular and colorful fan-favorite major league baseball players in the history of the game.

Berra shared about how he came to play with the New York Yankees. "I idolized Joe Medwich, the St. Louis Cardinal's outfielder, part of the Gashouse Gang. He was the man I watched. Know why I liked him a lot? I had a paper corner in St. Louis, he gave me a two-cent tip. I thought he was a heck of a guy!" He continued, "The Cardinals signed Joe for $500 a month and I wanted the same thing and they wouldn't give it to me so I signed with the Yankees instead." I always say that everything happens for a reason. The reason was clear to me as Yogi shared this story. He was supposed to play with the Yankees and it's as simple as that.

He was known for his humor by kidding-on-the-square when he would say things like, "It ain't over 'til it's over," "Ask me what time it is and I say 'now,'" "Nobody goes there, it's too crowded," "If there's a fork in the road, take it." Yogi said with a smile, "I don't know I say 'em, Mike."

I always wanted to know how Yogi got his nickname. He told me that, "Bobby Hoffman, second baseman for the Giants, we played on the same American Legion team and you know we didn't have any dugout. When we played then, we used to sit on the ground and I always had my legs crossed and my arms folded, and Bobby said, 'You look like a Yogi,' and it stuck after that."

I'll always remember the time when Yogi was invited to a Palm Springs ladies' luncheon as a guest speaker. He wanted to have another celebrity friend accompany him, so he called me and asked if I could join him.

To my complete dismay, I had committed to another engagement and wasn't able to go. It's something I will always regret and wished it was different, because of all the many celebrities and friends that Yogi had, he asked me. One of those things you never forget.

Yogi Berra, my pal, was an all-star of a man, on and off the field. I'm so happy we were on the same team when it came to friendship. His wife, Carmen died one year before Yogi. He passed away in 2015 at the age of 90 and I know, I just know he's still catching pitches in that big baseball stadium in the sky.

Pat Boone
Entertainer — Actor
Interviewed: 2002

I met Pat Boone many years ago at a celebrity charity golf tournament in Los Angeles, California. We had a lot in common such as entertainment, sports, playing golf and tennis. It wasn't long before I was invited to play tennis at his home in Beverly Hills. He had a hardcourt surface tennis court and occasionally invited his friends to play men's doubles and mixed doubles. We would also see each other at The Frank Sinatra Invitational and The Dennis James Celebrity Charity Tournaments in the Palm Springs and Los Angeles areas. Pat invited me to his golf tournament in Chattanooga, Tennessee, benefiting children of prisoners. Through the proceeds from the tournament, the children were given a home to live in with temporary guardians, food, clothing and special education tutoring, until their parent was released.

I still see Pat every year at the Tim Barry Irish Open Celebrity Golf Classic in Palm Desert, California. He has supported countless charitable organizations throughout the country, until this present day. Pat is a joy to be around, he always has a smile on his face, was good for a few jokes and had something interesting to say. He is highly intelligent with a strong patriotic sense about him. "I think it's a 'paculy' (his own word) American thing to figure out a way to have fun, get with people, even have music and all that and then raise lots and lots of money, hundreds of thousands, sometime eventually millions of dollars, to help other people. It's a genius thing and I love it."

Pat and I used wonderful health and skin care products from the same company, MDR, owned by Pat Riley. The product we liked the most was Vital Factors. It's full of nutrients and supplements that fortify the body and keep the mind sharp. Perhaps that explains how well Pat looks today, having used Vital Factors for so many years.

My wife, Mary Jane and I still see him on television infomercials for MDR, promoting the products and a very successful spokesperson for many other products, as well.

Pat Boone's musical history spans from recording gospel albums, hit songs from movies, to country songs, R & B and Pop. Pat remembered, "In my case, the first time on the charts

was 'Bernadine' and 'Love Letters in the Sand.' Both sides were my first hits." He added, "Kids generally grew up liking whatever their parents liked, whatever they were exposed to. In my case, it was Bing Crosby; my folks loved Bing. So, I loved hearing his music and trying to sing like Bing and sort of patterning my approach to entertainment on him."

Pat's records and albums have sold millions of copies throughout the world. His books, *Twixt 12 and 20* and *A New Song* have also sold more than two million copies.

His career began when he won the national competition on the Ted Mack Amateur Hour and the Arthur Godfrey Talent Scout show. After initial recordings of "Ain't That a Shame" and "I Almost Lost My Mind," 20th Century Fox Studios signed Boone to a film contract and ABC gave him his own weekly television program, *The Pat Boone Chevy Showroom*.

Pat appeared in approximately fifteen movies, including *State Fair* with the hit song, "April Love," *Mardi Gras, Journey to the Center of the Earth, All Hands on Deck, The Main Attraction, The Greatest Story Ever Told* and *The Cross and The Switchblade*, produced by his Cooga Mooga Film Production Corporation. "By the end of 1957, I was actually in the top ten box-office at the movies." Pat's success in films was second only to his success on vinyl. "For almost five years I was never off the charts. Not one week. It's one distinction I do hold in the record business today and that is over 200 consecutive weeks on the singles charts, without never being off."

Pat Boone is the author and co-author of sixteen books. One book in particular, *A Miracle Saved My Family*, published by Oliphants in 1971, revealed Boone's own marital life that fell prey to difficulty. Another book that he applied to his Christian beliefs to, with an emphasis on the problems of teenagers and family life, *Twixt 12 and 20,* has sold more than 800,000 copies with $1 million in royalties going to the North Eastern Institute for Christian Education. Very interesting to note and I'm sure the subject for another book that he could write, Pat mentioned he was a descendant of Daniel Boone.

Some of the many awards received by Boone include Personality of the Year by Variety Clubs of America, U.S. Junior Chamber of Commerce Award as one of ten outstanding young men, Catholic Youth Organization Celebrity Award, for edifying influence on the youth of America in the field of entertainment and the Brotherhood Award of the National Association of Christians and Jews.

My friend Pat Boone is an example of a true American who loves his country and appreciates his many God given talents. He has maintained the image of so much success humbly, through his Christian faith. I always look forward to seeing him with his smiling Irish eyes, his infectious smile and his love for life.

Pat tells us, "There is more, another dimension to this whole thing called the Christian life. But it only happens if you want it to. God won't cause it to happen if you don't want it to. He sums it up by saying, 'Live as we were created to live.'"

Eric Braeden
Actor
Interviewed: 1996

IT WAS QUITE A WHILE AGO when I first met actor Eric Braeden at one of the celebrity charity tennis tournaments in Los Angeles, California. We continued to play tennis socially at various friend's tennis courts in and around the Beverly Hills, California area. For the most part, we played doubles with and against other actors, directors and producers. We played singles on occasion, and Eric played better than I did, but it was always pleasantly competitive. In 1976, I invited Eric, along with quite a few Hollywood stars, to participate in my own celebrity charity tennis tournament in my hometown of Stamford, Connecticut. We had a great time and raised a lot of money for underprivileged children. It was tennis that brought us together for a good workout, to socialize and to raise money to benefit charitable causes.

Eric Braeden was born in Kiel, Germany and made his way to Hollywood via New York, Texas and Montana. He landed a partial track scholarship to Montana State University and there he combined his studies with the night shift at a local lumber mill. A fellow student invited him on a boat trip up the jagged Salmon River in Idaho and the two men were to become the first to survive the trip both up and down river. They filmed their journey and called the documentary *The Riverbusters*. Eric and his partner made their way to Los Angeles to find a distributor for the film and Braeden decided to stay on. During his stay, he joined a local semi-professional soccer team. He heard among some of his friends that German actors were being sought for various television and film projects. Braeden got an agent and suddenly found himself with a new career, one that he had wanted to try since he was in his teens.

Eric's first role was in the film, *Operation Eichmann* and in 1965 he appeared on Broadway in *The Great Indoors* with Curt Jurgens and Geraldine Page. The following year he was cast as Captain Dietrich on *The Rat Patrol* series, onboard for the next two years.

Upon leaving that show, he landed a starring role in the film *Colossus: The Forbin Project*. Films that followed were *The Ultimate Chase, Moritori, Honeymoon with a Stranger, A Hundred Rifles,* and *Escape from* the *Planet of the Apes*. He also made guest appearances in approximately one hundred and twenty television shows and was seen in a number of television movies including *The Judge and Mrs. Wyler, Happily Ever After* and *The Cry of the Rooster*.

In 1980, Braeden got a plum role in the hugely popular daytime CBS soap opera, *The Young and the Restless,* playing the suave Victor Newman. He reminded us that the hours of work on the set are long. "From a point of view of pure work, we do eighty pages, an entire script in one day. A night time TV show shoots about nine to ten pages a day; a film as you know, probably two to three pages a day. So the amount of work is extraordinary." Forty plus years later, Eric still appears on the show and maintains his suave, handsome stature. He shared his thoughts. "So many people watch soaps. It's unbelievable how many and what is further unbelievable is how many people, how many across the entire social stratum, and from rich to poor. So, it is truly a cultural phenomenon."

In 1991, Braeden was awarded the Federal Medal of Honor by the president of Germany in recognition of his achievements promoting a positive, realistic image of Germans in America while advancing German/Jewish dialogue. He co-founded the German-American Cultural Society for the same purposes after having been the only actor appointed to the German-American Advisory Board. The illustrious group included Dr. Henry Kissinger, Katharine Graham, Gen. Alexander Haig, Steffi Graf and Paul Volcker.

"I formed the German-American Cultural Society in order to engage in dialogue primarily with American and Jewish groups and I found that the outcome of that is very positive and encouraging. We need to discover what we have in common as human beings," he said.

Eric maintained an athletic regimen, playing soccer, skiing, jogging and tennis. We haven't seen each other for many years, but I often think of the good times we had on the tennis court and in show business. Eric was very gracious during our interview, eager to share the highlights of his life and career in Hollywood and around the world, known to so many as Victor Newman.

He expressed his take on being an actor, "The altruistic aspect of what we do as actors, is to entertain people. In daytime, you have characters that are closer to reality in the sense that they show 'grey' sides; sometimes good, sometimes bad. You resemble real figures far more than you do at night. That is the attraction of daytime, that you expose yourself emotionally."

Eric Braeden has entertained so many people, so well, for so long.

Dick Butkus
Actor – National Football League – Hall of Fame
Interviewed: 2000

I met National Football League Hall of Famer Dick Butkus when he invited me to play in his celebrity golf tournament for Serra Retreat in Malibu, California. It was a fun time and played to a full field. Dick hosted his tournament for four years along with several other tournaments throughout the country, that all benefitted greatly from his efforts to raise funds for each charity.

Dick shared that growing up, he loved watching movies and was inspired to get into the business. He especially identified with a fighter he saw in a film. Dick remarked on his inspiration growing up, "I used to watch movies a lot. Old movies where the young fighter comes from nowhere and he made it to the top." Dick made it to the top too, exceeding in football, in films, on TV and commercials. As my mom would say, "He did good!"

Butkus was an All-American selection while at the University of Illinois in 1963 and 1964. He led his team to the Big Ten Championship in 1963 with a 17–7 victory over Washington in the 1964 Rose Bowl. He was the Big Ten Most Valuable Player in 1963, Illinois Most Valuable Player in 1963 and 1964, also co-captained the 'Illini' in 1964. Butkus made first team All-Big Ten in his junior and senior years, named to the Big Ten Diamond Anniversary, 75th year team, in 1970, voted the *Sporting News* College Coaches All-Time Team and inducted into The College Hall of Fame in 1983.

Butkus went on to play nine years with the Chicago Bears from 1965 through 1973. Dick told us, "It's a big step. It's another test to see if you can make it from college to pro football. The biggest surprise was the incredible speed that pro football is to college."

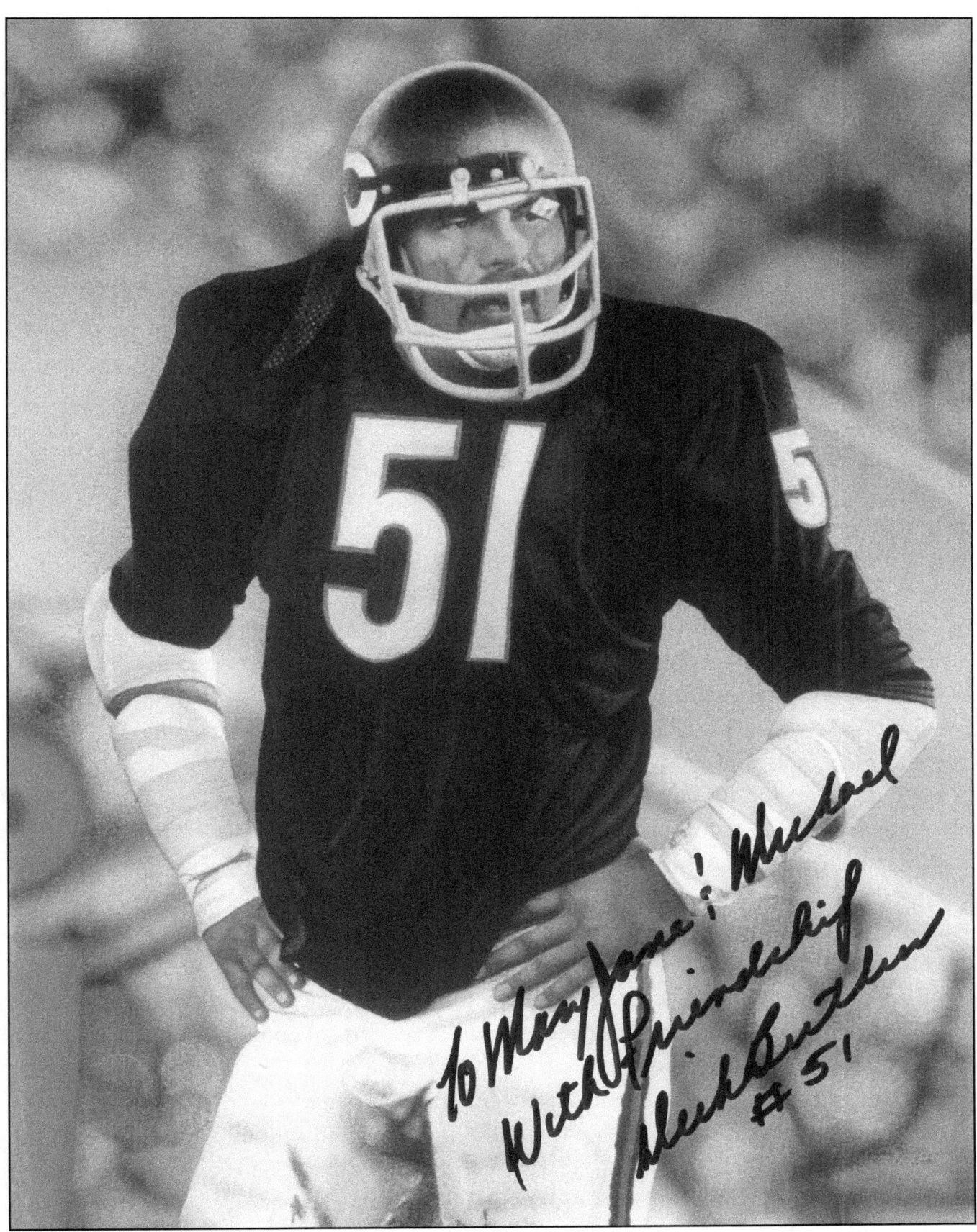

He continued, "On the field, the people are bigger, stronger and of course their skill levels are a lot better than they were in college. You're going up against the cream of the crop in the NFL."

He played in eight Pro-Bowls, named All-NFL linebacker seven of his nine years in the league, twice named The National Conference Defensive Player of the Year, named Pro-Football's All-Time Greatest Linebacker by fan vote, conducted by *The Sporting News*, the 1960s All-Decade Team by the Pro Football Hall of Fame, NFL All-Time Team, ESPN's 100 greatest players of the Century, *Sports Illustrated* with the Six Greatest Players of the Century and inducted into the Professional Football Hall of Fame in Canton, Ohio in 1979.

Dick's football career ended in 1973, after playing only nine games that season due to knee injuries. His interest in acting blossomed and he appeared in many films as the years rolled by. "Injuries took their toll; the knees were just gone. It's a long, long road and maybe you take the wrong fork in the road and don't make it. There's a sacrifice and a road to take with a lot of obstacles."

He appeared in such films as *Gus, Onion Man, Mother, Jugs and Speed, The Legend of Sleepy Hollow, Johnny Dangerously, Unnecessary Roughness, The Lawyer* and *The Last Boy Scout*. Butkus was a regular on several television series, *My Two Dads, Sports Analyst, NFL Today, Blue Thunder, Half Nelson, Suzuki's Great Outdoors, Butkus Awards* and *Hang Time*. Dick had roles in the television pilots, *A Matter of Life and Death, Timeout for Dad, Second City, Just One of the Girls, Gridiron* and the mini-series, *Rich Man, Poor Man*. Talking about his television series, "Our first series we did was *Blue Thunder*, then the next year a series called *Half Nelson* with Joe Pesci. My favorite series was *Hang Time*. I liked it because of the message."

Butkus's episodic performances were very impressive in *Wonder Woman, Dukes of Hazard, MacMillan and Wife, Six-Million Dollar Man, Magnum PI, Growing Pains, Murder She Wrote, Matlock, Saturday Night Live* and *Coach*.

He was interviewed on many popular radio shows, a sports commentator for WGN-Radio, sports commentator for WGSO, *Sports Shorts* and was in over two hundred television commercials.

Dick spoke about his experiences with commercials and film. "The Miller Lite commercials were fun. Because it was comedy and that's what I like to do. Let's get Bubba Smith and put these guys together on lots of commercials." The one thing he didn't like was when he went on an audition and they were late to see him. "Football, the thing you learn about discipline and time, you're there, no matter what, on time. In the casting waiting room, I always wanted to get up and leave when they were late."

Dick Butkus has great leadership qualities: humble, intelligent and grateful for all the God-given gifts he was blessed with. He was honored as a Football Hall of Famer and became a professional working actor. Those are the things dreams are made of. And those are the things he worked on, to make them come true.

Rory Calhoun
Actor
Interviewed: 1995

I FIRST MET RORY CALHOUN IN 1959 when I guest-starred in one of the popular *Desilu Playhouse* television segments entitled, *The Killer Instinct*. Rory did a fantastic job playing Joey Barnum, a real-life drama about a retired boxer who returns to the ring to teach his young protégé a valuable lesson. I had the pleasure of playing the young protégé, along with Rory and actress, Janice Rule.

It was one of my favorite roles in my entire career. As a matter of fact, the next day, in less than 24 hours later, I had two major contracts waiting for me as a result of my performance on that show. From the first day we met on the set, to the last scene of the show, it could not have been a better experience. Rory Calhoun was the most unselfish actor I ever worked with, only to include the great Robert Taylor. As the stars of their shows, they allowed the other actors more close-ups. In several scenes Rory said to the director, "Keep the camera on Michael, he's doing such a great job." Rory then turned to me and said, "You know a play, pictures or television is not a one-person show. You gonna have two people and if you give one guy a close-up or a lady a close-up, you gotta come around and reverse it so you got two people working together. That's how the whole thing is done."

When we finished the shoot, we kept in touch and stayed friends, until the day he passed away in 1999 at the age of 76.

Rory Calhoun began his illustrious career in the 1940s for 20th Century- Fox Studios. In 1993, he co-starred in the Warner Bros. movie entitled, *Pure Country* and that was 76 films later! Among the many pictures he co-starred in through the years was *The Red House*. Rory said, "Edward G. Robinson, we did *The Red House* together. It got me started. Delmer Daves was the producer, writer and director. Delmer Daves, did you know, was a rock collector? He delved into etymology (the origin of names and words) and geology. He used to cut and polish rocks. In *The Red House*, he made me carry back 900 pounds of rocks, and I blew out two tires in the trunk of my car!"

Rory starred and co-starred in the following films: *River of No Return* with Marilyn Monroe, *The Spoilers, Hired Gun*, a film he wrote, produced and starred in, *How to Marry a Millionaire, With a Song in My Heart, The Return of The Frontiersman, Rogue River, Miraculous Journey, I Climbed the Highest Mountain*, and the list goes on and on.

About Marilyn Monroe, Calhoun said, "She had a great big heart and a lovely soul. There was a great softness to her that a lot of people never saw. I had the flu during the filming of *River of No Return* and Marilyn put cool compresses on my brow and fed me soup for five days."

Rory was the first Hollywood actor to star in a 'spaghetti western' when independent producer Sidney Pink made the film, *Finger on The Trigger* in Spain. It started a rush of American actors seeking work in Spain and Italy. Rory worked with many of the finest actors and the most beautiful actresses in show business such as, Edward G. Robinson, Robert Mitchum, Jeff Chandler, Susan Hayward, Betty Grable, Lauren Bacall, Jean Tierney, Marilyn Monroe and many other big stars of the era.

Calhoun, starred in and co-produced the highly successful television series, *The Texan*, for three seasons, with his producer-partner Vic Orsatti. He spoke about the series with a smile, "I wrote 15 of 'em." I had the good fortune to be in four of those segments, back-to-back, and once again we enjoyed working together.

Rory also starred in the popular daytime soap opera, *Capitol*, for five years, playing the patriarch Judson Taylor. He also starred in two mini-series, *The Blue and the Gray* for CBS and *The Rebels* for Universal Studios.

His career began to evolve into character with comedy roles, starting with the Hollywood spoof, *Won Ton Ton – The Dog That Saved Hollywood*, and continued with the western comedy, *Mule Feathers*, followed by *Motel Hell*, the zany horror movie, playing a deranged character, Farmer Vincent. *Motel Hell* was a huge success and is regarded as a cult classic. The film *Angel* with Rory portraying a sympathetic crazy old coot, Kit Carson, was another big hit at the box office and earned him critical acclaim.

Rory's nickname was 'Smokey' because he constantly smoked cigarettes and eventually it took him from us, much too soon. I will always fondly remember working with him and the fun times my wife and I had spending Easter Sunday with he and his family for several years. Special memories of a special friend that we will always treasure.

Rory wanted our listeners to know, "I think my fate was the acting. I was never what you call a big star, I was never quite at that pinnacle. But I was always very comfortable just under it 'cause I didn't have to watch anybody coming up and try to knock me out of my shoes or something."

And for all who work in the entertainment industry, it's a point that's well taken.

Glen Campbell
Singer – Entertainer
Interviewed: 1996

I met Glen Campbell when we both attended a star-studded golf tournament and dinner benefiting The Mickey Mantle Donor Awareness Foundation in Las Vegas, Nevada. He entertained us that night and was sensational, as usual, to a standing ovation. It was a two-day tournament with two celebrities on each team of five, playing scramble golf. I had the pleasure of pairing with Glen the second day and we talked a great deal. He and I played to the same handicap and contributed a lot of good shots for our team. As I recall, we finished fourth or fifth, just below the three winning places. He had a great sense of humor and we shared stories throughout the day. Glen was a good golfer and was serious about improving his game.

Glen Campbell began his career playing guitar at the age of four and by the time he was six, he was an accomplished picker. At fourteen, he joined his uncle's three-piece band and later toured the Southwest with his own group before moving to Los Angeles, California at the age of twenty-four. He immediately found studio work playing on records for Frank Sinatra, Nat King Cole, Merle Haggard and Elvis Presley. In 1961, he released a single on a regional label that caused Capitol Records to sign him as an artist.

Glen told the story that the head of A&R at Capitol Records, Royal Gilmore, asked Glen, "What would you like to do?" He answered, "I wanna do what I wanna do. Just to sit down with my guitar and four or five pieces in the studio and play and sing what I want to play and sing. Here I am trying to please somebody who don't play or sing. The first thing I did was 'Gentle On My Mind.'"

Shortly thereafter, 1967 was a landmark year for Glen as a solo performer. In July of that year, "Gentle on My Mind" was released and became an overnight success and one of the most played songs in the history of country music. A series of hits followed, "By the Time I Get to Phoenix," "Wichita Lineman," "Hey Little One," "Galveston," "Rhinestone Cowboy"

Glen Campbell

GLEN CAMPBELL

and "Southern Knights." Glen told us, "Don Ho introduced him to the song "Galveston." Don sang it in a slow tempo and I upped the tempo and it became one of my biggest hits."

Glen Campbell landed his own television show, *The Glen Campbell Goodtime Hour* for CBS. He gave us a few behind-the-scenes tidbits about the show. "The writers that they had, Steve Martin, Rob Reiner, to name a few, McClain Stevenson was a writer on the show. It was so easy, easy to do. They didn't write a show and Glen Campbell in it. They wrote a show around what I did, a song, a skit or whatever."

He co-starred with John Wayne in the 1969 film, *True Grit* and sang the title song of the same name., as well. Glen made history by winning a Grammy Award in both country and pop music in 1967 for "Gentle on My Mind" and "By the Time I Get to Phoenix." He continued with more gold records, "Try A Little Kindness," "Rhinestone Cowboy" and "Southern Knights." He sold more than forty-five million records, earning eleven gold albums, four gold singles and five Grammy Awards.

Campbell's ongoing association with New Haven Records, performing gospel music, won him a Dove Award and a new following. He continued recording with a very successful video, *No More Nights*, released to the Christian market, which was received with critical acclaim. Glen shared, "I loved doing the Christian albums."

Glen enjoyed owning and performing at his own venue in Branson, Missouri, The Glen Campbell Theater. "It's a 2,200 seat theater and it's just awesome; sound, best sound I've ever played anywhere. The people that built the theater did a great job. It was used for charity benefits, as well." The entertainment continuously played to packed houses and standing ovations, whatever the occasion.

Glen's autobiography, *Rhinestone Cowboy* was a collaborative effort with writer Tom Carter, that produced an enlightening and exciting tale of his life. He was one of the greatest singers and entertainers throughout the world and will always be remembered for his gifted, pleasantly unique voice. Glen's award winning musical achievements were silenced when he passed away at age 81 in 2017.

It was a true gift for me to spend that quality time with this legend of song. Thank you, Glen Campbell for all your talent and your friendship.

Rosie Casals

Women's Tennis Association — Tennis Hall of Fame

Interviewed: 2007

THE FIRST TIME I MET ROSIE CASALS was at the Indian Wells Tennis Gardens in Indian Wells, California. I was invited to play in a celebrity mixed doubles match and Rosie and I were tennis partners. It was intensely competitive and we had fun rallying back and forth and she played at just the right pace to make it entertaining. Rosie, affectionately known by her friends as 'Rosebud,' was born and raised in San Francisco, California. She learned to play tennis, taught by her father, Manuel, on the public courts at Golden Gate Park. Rosie shared about her early life in tennis, "As I progressed in my 10, 12, 14 years divisions, winning most of them, I was ranked No. 1 in Northern California, so I knew I had something going for myself and it was great being able to win the tournaments. I came from a background that wasn't that spectacular. We were poor financially but I didn't realize until later how rich I was in a lot of things."

Rosie found fame in the 1960s and '70s, when she became one of the women's top five players for the first time in 1964 and remained there for eleven consecutive years. Her career highlights included seven Wimbledon doubles and mixed doubles titles; five with Billie Jean King and two with Elie Nastase, including the Italian, Australian and Open doubles champion. In 1970, Rosie was the winner of the first ever Virginia Slims Tournament and the first winner of the Family Circle Cup in 1973, when she received $30,000. It was the highest purse ever awarded to a female athlete at that time. Rosie said, "Just to clarify things, professional tennis came into the picture in 1968. That was the first time that really contracted women and we were paid a guarantee. As we know, professional tennis was born in 1968."

Rosie was one of the founders of the Women's Tennis Association along with Billie Jean King and the Original Nine. They were the moving force in establishing equality and

bringing recognition to women's tennis on the Virginia Slims circuit and in the tennis arena, as a whole. Rosie reflected on the details of her professional association with Billie Jean King, "I think it was a combination. Certainly, Billie Jean at the time, because she was number one at the time, her voice was the loudest. Myself, I was there along her side and I think we were very instrumental because I'm very vocal. And even though a lot of the time we didn't agree on how to get there, but ultimately, we were able to rally the rest of the players to come and support the idea of collectively uniting."

Casals was the color commentator along with Howard Cosell for the highly publicized Battle of the Sexes between Billie Jean King and Bobby Riggs at the Houston Astrodome in 1973. In 1995, Rosie was inducted into the Marin County Tennis Hall of Fame and in 1996 at the International Tennis Hall of Fame in Newport, Rhode Island. She was also inducted into the Bay Area Sports Hall of Fame in 2003, with John Elway, Willie Shoemaker and Tom Meschery.

Rosie played in many invitational tennis events, but spent most of her time with her company, Sportswoman, which she established in 1982 to organize and promote the 'over thirties' Tennis Classic Tour, which ran from 1983 through 1987. In 2002, she joined forces with Bay area artist Bruce Lattig and formed Sports Art, to market spectacular watercolor portraits and limited edition prints of past legends and today's greatest tennis players.

Sportswoman was the coordinator for the Harbor Point Charitable Foundation's tennis events. She also assisted in the 2005 and 2006 Tennis Classics charity event benefitting Celebrate Life Breast Cancer Foundation and Youth Tennis Advantage.

Casals coordinated the Billie Jean King and Friends Tennis Fundraiser for Cal State, Los Angeles, benefitting the athletic scholarship programs and the women's tennis team. Over the years they have raised well over one million dollars.

Rosie 'Rosebud' Casals has always been a driving force in women's tennis and many charitable events that benefit women's causes. She is a champion on and off the tennis court and it was my honor to interview Rosie and talk about her career achievements and her humanitarian contributions.

Casals told us about Wimbledon, "There's nothing like center court. Wimbledon to me, as a player, is the ultimate. There's nothing like it. Outside of the French Open, I don't think there's another tournament that exists like Wimbledon."

12

Norm Crosby
Entertainer
Interviewed: 1996

I MET ENTERTAINER NORM CROSBY many years ago when our close friends, Jerry and Rita Vale, introduced us and we've been friends ever since. We both loved playing golf and were invited to the same charity tournaments throughout Los Angeles and the Palm Springs, California desert area. We also became part of the 'Celebrity Lunch Bunch' that met each week day at the Café Roma Restaurant in Beverly Hills, California. It was an interesting and eclectic group of show business colleagues that included actors, singers, comedians, producers, directors, writers and production coordinators and we all shared our stories, always with humor. Truly, Café Roma was like our second home. Norm was a very intricate part of the entertainment of our group because he always had new jokes to share with us after he came back from being on the road.

It's interesting to know that Norm didn't pursue a career in comedy. "No, I never, ever aspired to comedy. As a matter of fact, I was a commercial artist. That's what I did. But I fooled around with comedy because I enjoyed it. That's the way it starts. You do it for fun." Norm added, "Just to be funny so that you ease the burden of daily living, which is a pain in the neck for everybody."

When I moved from Beverly Hills to the Palm Springs area, I hosted my own golf tournament, The Michael Dante Celebrity Charity Golf Classic, for eight years. Norm was always invited to participate and play golf, but he was also gracious, offering to be a part of the entertainment program. He was so funny and brought down the house every time he performed. For many years, I played in his tournament benefiting the Muscular Dystrophy Association in Industry Hills, California and the Annual Norm Crosby City of Hope Tournament, as well.

Norm Crosby is the master of the malapropism; the confusion of words that are similar in sound, and he is among the most recognized and widely quoted performers in show business. "I started in the business as a 'club date act.' I never worked in a nightclub. I started doing convention dates and banquets." He continued, "If people can identify with your humor, if they can recognize the situations that you talk about, then it's easy."

Crosby was one of the busiest of the classic, big name comedians in the nation's best theaters and casino showrooms, on the banquet circuit, as well as the top television variety, talk and game shows. He served as Jerry Lewis' co-host on Jerry's Annual Labor Day Telethon for the Muscular Dystrophy Association with Norm presiding over the show's national live remote segments from Los Angeles. Norm has hosted television talk shows, game shows, variety and awards specials, as well as his own series, *Norm Crosby's Comedy Shop.*

Some years ago, the Anheuser-Busch company decided to use that "Likeable guy who talks funny" to do a commercial for natural light beer. The results were excellent and after many subsequent commercials, Norm was made a corporate spokesman for all Anheuser-Busch products. Because of a hearing affliction, Crosby has a special interest in the problems of the hearing impaired. He is a trustee of The Hope for Hearing Foundation at UCLA and he was appointed by President Ronald Reagan as his special ambassador for Better Hearing and Speech Month. He has also been a heavy fundraiser and tireless worker for the City of Hope, the internationally famous hospital and medical research facility in Duarte, California. Crosby is also a national ambassador for Childhelp USA, and joined First Lady Barbara Bush in Washington, D.C. to launch National Child Abuse Prevention Month. He has served, for several years as the City of Hope's International Ambassador of Good Will.

Norm talked about performing on my show, stating that comedy shows threw everything at him but the kitchen sink.

"There is nothing conceivable, Michael, that would happen to me on the floor, that I wouldn't know how to get out of. I've seen fire, fist fights, the lights go off, a waitress drops a whole tray of dishes. That's what makes you powerful on the stage. It's the confidence, the peace of mind, the security of knowing that I know what I'm doing up here."

In recognition of his achievements, both in comedy and as a humanitarian, the Hollywood Chamber of Commerce installed his star on Hollywood's Walk of Fame in 1982. In 1991, Norm received the Victory Award from President George Bush at the Kennedy Center Awards Gala in Washington, D.C.

Norm Crosby's star will always shine bright for me as my friend, a man with incredible comedic talent and as a dedicated humanitarian from his heart. "I guess everybody in our business, some way or another gets involved with charity things, with projects. It's a way,

Michael, of giving back a little. It's a way of saying thank you for the lives we lead, for the success we enjoy."

And I thank you, Norm for your friendship and I will always remember your smiling face. Norm passed away in 2020 at the age of 93.

13

Tony Curtis
Actor – Artist
Interviewed: 1995

I FIRST MET TONY CURTIS in the late 1950s at Nicky Blair's house for a bachelor's dinner in the Hollywood Hills in Los Angeles, California. Nicky was an actor for many years and then became a well-known restauranteur in Los Angeles. Tony and Nicky were very good friends and both started their acting careers when they got out of the military in the mid-1940s. When they arrived in Hollywood, they met and shared an apartment until Tony signed a contract with Universal Studios. They went their separate ways, but remained close friends throughout their lives.

Nicky was a very popular personality in Hollywood and I dare say he knew more people in show business than anyone. He and his business partner owned Nicky Blair's, a wildly successful restaurant on Sunset Boulevard, and a favorite hangout for actors, directors and producers. Tony, another actor friend of ours, Perry Lopez, and I met often at Nicky's restaurant for dinner. Tony had a great sense of humor and loved to tease Nicky throughout the evening. We all met there for a long time until Nicky closed the restaurant and retired from the restaurant business in the 1990s.

It didn't take long for Tony's career to get rolling. He was handsome, talented, charming with a bundle of energy that could only be claimed by a few of his peers. Tony told me about the studio contract system on my radio show.

"If you weren't under contract it would be very hard for you to get even a bit part in a movie because each studio had its' couderay, (French for group of or selection of) so to speak, of actors and actresses, Tony said. "The system created itself. But it was a great opportunity for us as young actors."

Tony went on to star in more than one hundred films including, *The Defiant Ones*, which earned him an Academy Award nomination for Best Actor.

Some of his other films included *Trapeze, The Sweet Smell of Success, Some Like It Hot, Spartacus, Operation Petticoat, The Boston Strangler, Houdini, The Great Imposter, The Great*

Race, Taras Bulba, and many more. I mentioned those films because every characterization was so different from the other. His versatility was one of his strengths and I never saw Tony play anything 'safe' as actors say, because he had the courage and talent to take chances as an actor, and make it all work, for over six decades.

While his hair turned gray, he still projected that same energy on television that he brought to the big screen throughout his career. Curtis starred in the British made series entitled, *The Persuaders* and later in *McCoy,* among several other carefully selected dramatic guest roles. He said, "Television makes everything a quick soundbite. In films, things open and close much quicker than they used to because television makes it more pertinent."

Tony starred in a feature film for director Martin Scorsese called, *Naked in New York,* followed by two international television projects, hosting a twenty-six-episode series of Hollywood stories entitled, *Hollywood Babylon,* which was syndicated around the world. He hosted the first of an Annual Magic Awards Show, *Magic Star,* that was shot in Tokyo for international release. Curtis became a major international figure in the world of magic when he starred in the motion picture *Houdini* and continued to present his own shows in such venues as the famed Magic Castle in Hollywood.

While Tony had been a major presence on the big screen and on television throughout the years, he had also managed to maintain another career in the arts, developing his love for the art of the canvas into a success that propelled him headlong into the art world.

Exhibitions of his original artwork showcased in Hawaii and other locations in the United States, as well as Japan, England, Hungary and Canada. Curtis accumulated more than $5 million in sales, making him among the most collected artists of his generation. About his artwork, Tony said, "I've been a painter, a drawing person all my life. I'm always drawing."

Throughout all of his successes, Curtis retained his natural charm and a sense of an international bon vivant. He was an international traveler, feeling at home in every capital of the world, many of which he had made films in. His experiences helped to develop him into a writer, an artist and a philosopher of world cultures, as well as a romantic idol to beautiful women everywhere. Explaining his life, Tony shared with me and my listening audience, "Filmmaking is OK, but it's not my life, it isn't everything; it's one stone in the mosaic of my life." His life's mosaic came to an end in 2010, at the age of 85.

He did something so thoughtful and dear for my wedding to Mary Jane in 1992. Tony sent us a magnificent bouquet of flowers; one of every kind in the floral shop. And the note said, "And they said it wouldn't last." Although he couldn't be at our wedding in person, he was in spirit and artistry, through his flowers that were there.

I will always remember the wonderful work he brought to the screen, his canvas art, his energy, intelligence, his sense of humor, and above all, his friendship.

Beryl Davis
Singer – Entertainer
Interviewed: 1994

I MET SINGER-ENTERTAINER-RECORDING ARTIST Beryl Davis at a social gathering with friends in Palm Springs, California. She was very charming, with an effervescent personality. During our conversation that evening, I mentioned my radio show and she said she heard the show and especially liked the questions I asked my guests. She graciously accepted and a week later we rendezvoused and enjoyed the interview, while getting to know each other better. Beryl was aware of my career in show business and was very impressed by my success, as I was of hers.

Beryl Davis was destined to be a big band singer. She was the daughter of English bandleader, Harry Davis. She was born on the road, so to speak, during one of her father's tours and spent many of her formative years traveling with the band throughout England. She grew up to be an accomplished singer and during World War II, she caught the eye and ear of the great band leader, Glenn Miller who had come to England in 1942, as part of the war effort. Once established, Miller went searching for a female singer to accompany his group and hired Davis. "He enlisted me," said Beryl, with a smile. She remembered traveling across England to perform amid bombs, blitzes and fighter attacks. Davis continued to sing with Miller, although American General James Doolittle made her a member of Special Forces attached to the Eighth Air Force, the only British civilian ever to receive such an honor.

Davis took orders from General Doolittle to never travel outside of England, when Miller traveled abroad. That stay-at-home policy included the time Miller and the band flew to Paris on a military flight, December 15, 1944. They left England but didn't arrive at their destination in France. Investigators never discovered their fate, presuming that enemy fire shot down Miller's plane.

After the war, Davis settled in the United States and performed with Bob Hope and delighted audiences singing her hit record, "I'll Be Seeing You," that she performed around

the world promoting the Big Band sound. She toured with the Big Band Salute to Glenn Miller along with performing with the Modernaires with Paula Kelly Jr, Dick Haymes Jr., and Rex Allen with his orchestra. Davis said she continued to be amazed and pleased by the attention the big band sound had received. "There are many people who find that there's something to be gained by looking back." She named singer Harry Connick Jr, as a singer-musician who popularized the music of yesterday, thanks to his remake of "It Had to Be You," from the *When Harry Met Sally* soundtrack.

Davis entertained on the road all her life, crisscrossing the globe with her talent as a song stylist. She appreciated both her newer, younger fans and those fans who had been with her from the beginning. "It was something more than music, particularly when I performed for World War II Veterans. We invoked the memories and it showed them how much they loved the music of that time." "As for myself," Beryl said, "It's been a fabulous roller coaster ride of life."

Her life of song and entertainment gave so many so much joy, until her passing at age 87 in 2011.

Ann Meyers Drysdale
Women's National Basketball Association – Hall of Fame
Interviewed: 2001

THE FIRST TIME I MET ANN MEYERS DRYSDALE was at the Frank Sinatra Invitational in Palm Springs, California. She was one of only a few celebrity lady golfers participating in the tournament and was quite good at the game. Ann played in the golf tournament every year and was very popular among all the celebrity guests and patrons. Several years later when she was married to baseball's major league Hall of Famer, Don Drysdale, I introduced Ann to my wife Mary Jane at a Los Angeles Dodgers' game when her husband was pitching against the Cincinnati Reds. We have been friends ever since, exchanging holiday greeting cards and seeing each other at special events in the desert from time to time.

Ann was the first woman inducted into the UCLA Hall of Fame and the Woman's Sports Hall of Fame in 1987, a member of the National Basketball Hall of Fame in 1993, and in 1999 was inducted into the Inaugural Class of the Women's Basketball Hall of Fame. Myers graduated from UCLA, a four-time All-American and led the Bruins to the 1978 AIA Women's Championship. She also played volleyball at UCLA and was a member of the 1975 UCLA Championship Track and Field Team. She participated on the Olympic team in 1976, who lost to the Soviets.

"In the '76 Olympics, we won the Silver. I say that with great pride. For me, there was nothing like it," Ann said. "To be an Olympian and an American to represent your country, that has always stood out for me. The pride to represent your country; the pride to be able to go out there and compete and you never know what's going to happen."

Ann also competed in the Pan-American team and the World Championship team in 1975 and 1979. In 1978, she was the first player drafted into the Women's Professional Basketball League. She was named the Most Valuable Player of the League in 1979 and 1980, while playing with the New Jersey Gems. The following year Meyers-Drysdale signed

with the NBA's Indiana Pacers, the only female player to ever do so. Ann shared with us, "I decided that I had an opportunity that most people don't get in a lifetime, to try out in the NBA. And the Indiana Pacers came through and that's when I tried out. When the Pacer thing came along, we worked out a deal that if I didn't make it as a player, I would do broadcasting and that's what happened."

Following her tryout with the Pacers, she began her broadcasting career as a part-time color commentator for the Indiana Pacers. Ann did the same for Prime Ticket, Sports Time and Sports Vision Channels. Since 1983, Ann served as an ESPN analysis for men's and women's NCAA Basketball and softball games, and covered the NCAA women's basketball tournament for ESPN since 1985, the network coverage of the Final Four since 1996, the Women's Basketball Association since 1997, college games on Fox since 1985, Prime's coverage of NCAA basketball, commentator for the NCAA men's and women's basketball championship, the Summer Olympics, the Goodwill Games, Women's National Basketball Association since 1997 and the Olympic Games in the year 2000 in Sydney, Australia.

Ann also signed to compete in the *Women's Superstars*. With a warm smile, Ann said, "Through the *Women's Superstars* I had won three in a row, but through that I met my future husband, Don Drysdale, who was broadcasting for ABC."

Ann was a dedicated wife to her superstar husband, is a loving mom to their three beautiful children and her family, as well as an outstanding athlete and superb announcer in all facets of women's basketball.

Ann is an example of excellence for all women's sports. Her philosophy about playing basketball, "There's alotta luck involved, but there's nothing like the experience of the tournament."

A superstar herself, Ann remains humble and sincere and best of all, for Mary Jane and me, our long-time friend. Our enjoyable interview ended with a great trivia question from her, "Who is the only family to have three championships in basketball?"

I think we all know the answer to that one.

James Farentino
Actor
Interviewed: 2003

I met award winning actor James Farentino in the early days of his arrival to Hollywood from New York, at Joe Allen's Restaurant on Melrose Avenue. 'Jimmy' as his friends called him, and I sat many nights at the same table talking about movies, actors, directors, sports, family and about our likes and dislikes in the world. Our mutual friend, fine actor Anthony Franciosa, who was married to actress Shelley Winters at the time, invited us to his home for an Italian dinner, which was cooked for us by his mom. Coincidently, Jimmy's mom was visiting with him from New York and my mom was visiting me from Connecticut. We asked Tony if we could bring our moms along. And he responded with joy, "My mom would love that and so would I, please do." It was an exceptionally fun night and we all enjoyed each other's company like family. As you would expect, the food was to die for and Tony, Shelley and his mom were the perfect hosts.

James Farentino came to Hollywood from the Broadway stage. His first Broadway show, *Night of The Iguana* starred Bette Davis. "It gave me the opportunity to study how actors worked and the disciplinarian approach to acting. It was a challenge; I had never done anything like this before. Audiences loved it."

Later, he went on to win awards for his terrific performances in *One Flew Over the Cuckoo's Nest* and *A Streetcar Named Desire*. He also played Biff Loman in *Death of a Salesman* opposite George C. Scott. On film, James starred in approximately twenty motion pictures including, *The War Lord, Ensign Pulver, Banning, Psycho Mania, Me Natalie, Rosie, The Final Countdown, Termination Man, Bulletproof, The Last Producer* and *Women of the Night*, to name just a few.

His movies of the week included *The Wings of Fire, The Sound of Anger, Longest Night, Crossfire, The Family Rico, The Possessed, Evita Peron, Silent Victory, A Summer to Remember,*

Picking Up the Pieces, Family Sins, Naked Lie, Honor Thy Father and Mother, Murders in The Mirror and *When No One Would Listen,* directed by his former wife, Michele Lee.

James received an Emmy nomination for best supporting actor for his role in Franco Zeffirelli's *Jesus of Nazareth*. My wife, Mary Jane and I watch *Jesus of Nazareth*, on each Easter, and we think it was one his finest performances. He spoke about his acting in the part, "There's a scene in the film where Simon Peter, he's converting, he's having a catharsis. He's going from a drunken fisherman to believing that Jesus is the Messiah." Zeffirelli gave James the license to explore his thoughts and feelings about that transition. He continued, "It's one of those enriching moments that you can't put your finger on and I'll never forget it. Maybe Zeffirelli knew something I didn't know. He was going in a certain direction and was giving me the trust. There was no written dialogue for the scene and it just happened to work."

James Farentino was a series regular on the television hit series, *Dynasty, Julie, Mary,* and *Blue Thunder* and he had recurring roles on *Melrose Place, ER* and *Police Story*. His guest appearances on episodic television were numerous in *Ironside, Laredo, The Alfred Hitchcock Hour. Run for Your Life, The Virginian, Ben Casey, The Fugitive, 12 o'clock High, The Defenders, 77 Sunset Strip, The FBI* and the list goes on.

Throughout Jimmy's illustrious career, he continued to appear on stage in *The Best Man* in Chicago, *A Thousand Clowns* at Burt Reynold's Theater in Florida, *The Big Knife, Goodbye Charlie, California Suite, The Days and Nights of Be-Be Fenstermaker, In the Summer, Love Letters* and *Boy Gets Girl* at the Geffen Playhouse in Westwood, California.

About *Boy Gets Girl* he said, "It's the first thing I've done in three years. It showed me that you never forget, you keep growing and if you don't ride a bicycle for five or ten years, you're still gonna get on a bicycle and do it well. You know and so that's what I realize about whatever talent I have, whatever I have to give to this craft, it doesn't leave me, it always grows as I grow as a human being, as I live longer and longer, hopefully. It was just a joy."

It was amazing that Jimmy always made time, in between all of his work on television, in movies and on the stage, to stay in touch with his friends, including me. Sadly, he passed away at age 73 in 2012 and left behind his words of wisdom, about what he did so well. "That's why I'm still in this business. I don't take it for granted anymore. It's loving me and I love it." But he added, "Everything I've ever done that was satisfactory or challenging to me or satisfying, was something I was very frightened of."

Rhonda Fleming
Actress
Interviewed: 2006

I met Rhonda Fleming many years ago at several social events in Beverly Hills, California. She was more exquisite in person than she was on the silver screen with her beautiful, charismatic presence. During our conversation, she asked if I would escort her to a formal occasion and of course, I accepted immediately. She looked so beautiful in the gorgeous dress she wore that evening, and couldn't have been nicer. I saw her a couple of times after that, but we both got very busy working in Hollywood. Time flew by and we went our separate ways. Rhonda appeared in over forty motion pictures, co-starring with some of the top stars in show business, such as Gregory Peck, Ingrid Bergman, Robert Mitchum, Kirk Douglas, Charlton Heston, Glenn Ford, Burt Lancaster, Bob Hope, Bing Crosby, Rock Hudson and made four films with Ronald Reagan. Some of those films were *Spellbound, Connecticut Yankee, Yankee Pasha, The Great Lover, The Last Outpost, Hong Kong, Pony Express, Inferno, Cry Danger, Eagle and The Hawk, Gunfight At the O.K Corral, Home Before Dark* and *The Big Circus.*

Rhonda spoke about some of the stars and directors she worked with, including Alfred Hitchcock. "My first role was in *Spellbound*. Alfred Hitchcock, he was, I would say my favorite director because he didn't tell me how to say anything. He left that to me because he liked the way I did it. He helped me a lot; he gave me that something extra that I wasn't familiar with."

Another memory Rhonda shared was about Ronald Reagan. "I made four films with Ronald Reagan, with lots and lots of love scenes. Do you think I ever dreamed I was kissing the President of the United States? He was a delight."

Rhonda added, "The one thing, more than anything, I regret? I had finished playing my time in Las Vegas at the Tropicana Hotel. Came home, had my gowns and my songs. It was Christmas and I was tired and I had the tree up for my mother and my son and we were going to celebrate. Bob (Hope) called me directly and he said, 'Rhonda, would you come overseas with me? Michael, I don't know where I was coming from. I turned Bob Hope down, but I said I couldn't. The biggest opportunity of my life could have been that." She added that, "Working with him and Bing (Crosby) were just two of the highlights of my life in those films."

Rhonda appeared on Broadway in *The Women* and *Kismet* at the Los Angeles Music Center and later made her stage musical debut in Las Vegas at the opening of the new Tropicana Hotel's showroom. Later she appeared at the Hollywood Bowl in a one-woman concert of

Cole Porter and Irving Berlin's compositions. Singing was and has remained her first love. During our interview, Rhonda and I shared a mutual life-threatening experience – almost drowning. It was during her 23-year marriage to theater mogul, Ted Mann, while vacationing in Jamaica. Rhonda went snorkeling with a group of tourists as Mann, who was not a swimmer, stayed on shore. She was so busy enjoying the underwater scenery that she soon found herself far behind the pack. "I looked back and saw Ted standing by himself on the beach and I thought I'd better get back as my breathing was getting tougher and I started to hyperventilate. I couldn't stay above water. It felt like two hands were pulling my feet and legs under and I cried out as loud as I could, 'Help me! Help me!' This is where, every time I tell this story, I get goose bumps and tears, because suddenly there was a man standing next to Ted and he was not there before."

Realizing Rhonda was in danger, Mann turned to the stranger and said, "Go! Go!" Rhonda continued, "The man came out to me so fast; he took me by the elbow and guided me to the shore." The man who saved Rhonda Fleming's life vanished as mysteriously as he appeared. He helped her regain her breathing and was gone!

Rhonda asked Ted later, "Where did he come from?" Ted replied, in awe, "I don't know." Rhonda told me, "I knew in my heart that the man was an angel. I have been saved so many times and it's by His grace that I'm here today. I think God intervened because he had a higher purpose for me."

Rhonda Fleming; the movie star, mother, grandmother, philanthropist, and humanitarian, along with Ted Mann, established the Rhonda Fleming-Mann Center for Comprehensive Care for Women with Cancer at UCLA and the Rhonda Fleming Research Fellowship at the City of Hope, to advance research and treatment associated with women's cancer.

Rhonda shared her personal philosophy. "To me the key to a rich inner life is love, the ability to love, to have love, to give love, to share love and to feel love. It's not always easy and it's not always reciprocal. Jesus taught us how to love. That's what he came for, because he is pure love."

Rhonda is responsible for the first media convention in the Roanoke Valley in Virginia. She created the Pointing North Publication, dedicated to Christian film and television stars and their many fans. The fans encouraged the start of the first convention, the RoVa Con in 1976.

I always admired her talent and her many philanthropic contributions. Rhonda Fleming is the 'forever beauty' that I was privileged to be acquainted with during the Golden Years of Hollywood.

In October 2020, Rhonda passed away at the age of 97, gently resting in the loving arms of her Lord.

18

Robert Forster
Actor
Interviewed: 2000

I MET ROBERT FORSTER MANY YEARS AGO at Joe Allen's, a famous actor's restaurant on Melrose Avenue in Hollywood, California. We were pals until his death at the age of 78 in 2019. Robert was one of the nicest guys, always friendly with a great smile on his handsome face. Robert was genuinely interested in what was going on in my life and we had a mutual respect for each other and each other's work.

A native of Rochester, New York, Robert began his career in local community theater before moving to New York City, where he made his professional debut in the two-character Broadway production of *Mrs. Dally Has a Lover*. His other stage appearances include, *A Streetcar Named Desire*, *The Glass Menagerie*, *12 Angry Men*, *The Sea Horse* and *One Flew Over the Cuckoo's Nest*.

Forster left Broadway to co-star in his first film with Marlon Brando and Elizabeth Taylor in, *Reflections in a Golden Eye*, directed by the great John Houston. Robert reminisced, "John Houston, he was terrific to me. Always helpful. Gave me a shot to work and try my wings out cause I'd never done it before. He was excellent to me. A good guy, John Houston." Many films followed including, *Stalking Moon*, a period western with Gregory Peck and Eva Marie Saint, *Medium Cool*, *Justine*, *The Don is Dead*, *Black Hole*, *Delta Force*, *29*, *Supernova*, *Rear Window*, *Psycho*, *Family Tree*, *The Magic of Marciano*, and the list goes on.

Robert starred in three television series, *Banyon*, *Once a Hero*, and *Nakia*. He appeared in two pilots, *Checkered Flag* and *Mickie and Frankie* plus five episodes of *Police Story*, for which he received an Emmy Award playing a tough detective.

Robert appeared on many episodic television shows and movies of the week such a, *Necessary Force*, *Death Squad*, *Royce*, *The City*, *Standing Tall*, *The Clone* and *Goliath Awaits*.

In 1985, he produced and directed *Hollywood Harry*, a detective film spoof in which he starred with his 14-year-old daughter, Katherine.

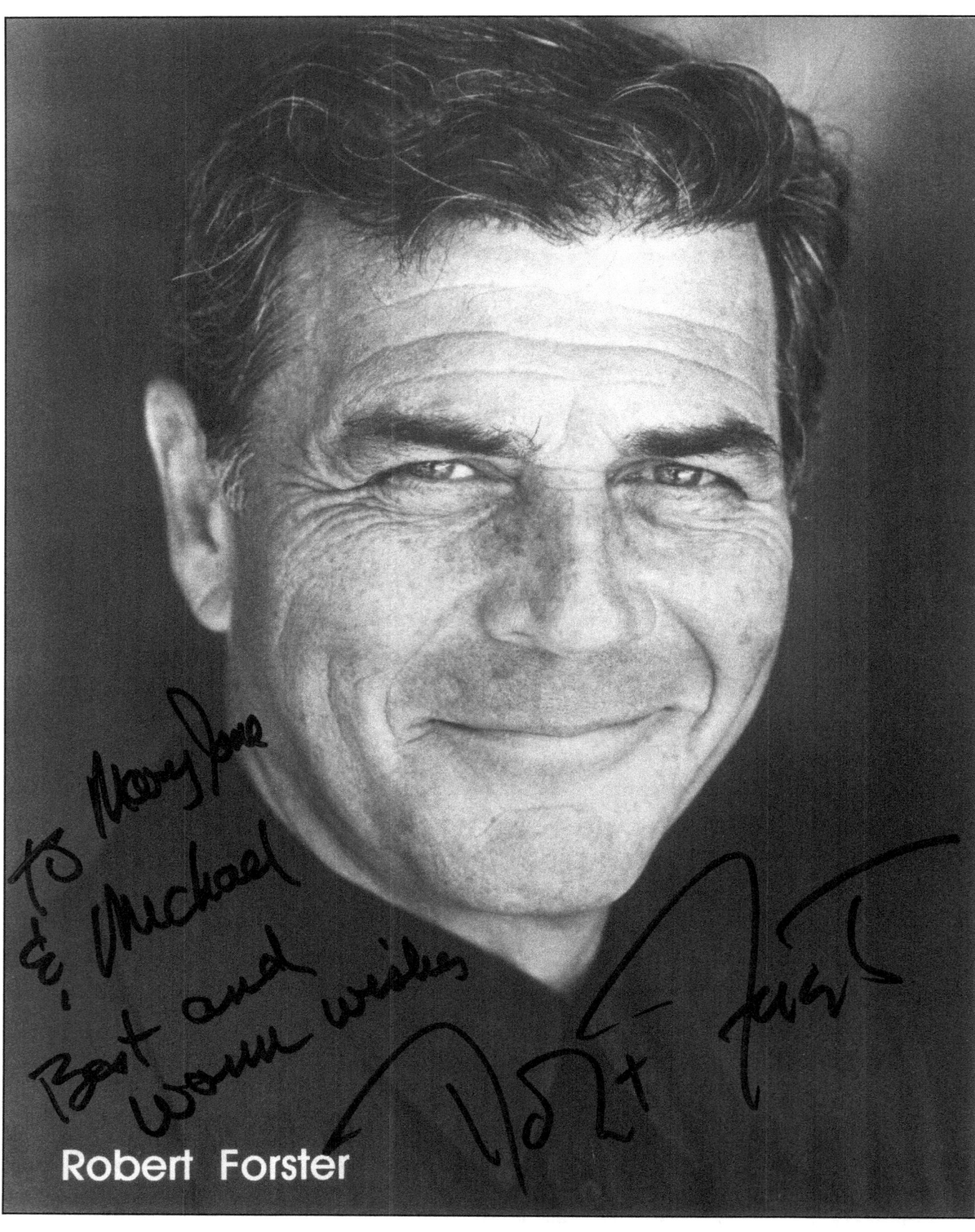

Forster's role as Detective Max Cherry in Quentin Tarantino's *Jackie Brown* was a made-to-order performance for Robert and helped to revive his career. About Tarantino, "He wrote me a wonderful, wonderful part in *Jackie Brown*. This is a gift the size you cannot exaggerate. I know that a lot of other actors, big stars wanted this role, but he decided he wanted to put me back to work. Can you imagine this?"

His characterization of Max Cherry garnered universal critical acclaim, but even more importantly, he received an Oscar nomination as Best Supporting Actor. The movie turned his career around, one that started well over thirty years before, suddenly putting him in great demand as an actor. His last fine performance was in 2019 in *El Camino – A Breaking Bad Movie*, the culmination of the *Breaking Bad Series* with Brian Cranston and Aaron Paul. He was a central character and outstanding in the film. Tragically, Robert died shortly before it aired at age 78.

When not performing in front of the camera, Robert was interacting as a motivational speaker, just like a standup comedy act, with a menu of positive stories instead of jokes. He spoke to various groups for free or to benefit charitable organizations.

Robert said, "And I say this, you can do any job and if you find the right thing to apply to any job of any kind and raise it to the level of an art form. You get that reward they always tell you, that you get when you deliver excellence to anything.

You get the reward of self-respect, respect from others and satisfaction that this is the real McCoy – this is un-transferable wealth. If you stick that reward in your pocket, it will always be there." Another of his motivational philosophies was, "If you are representing yourself, you can do anything you want. If you're representing somebody else, you really have to bring the best human being you got in you out, if you can, if you can."

I will always remember Robert Forster as a friend, a fine actor, but most of all, a caring, sensitive, wonderful human being.

Connie Francis
Entertainer – Actress
Interviewed: 2000

I FIRST MET CONNIE FRANCIS IN PALM SPRINGS, California, when she was singing in a popular nightclub. My wife, Mary Jane and I saw the show and went backstage to congratulate her on how well she performed. She was truly sensational. During our conversation, I asked if I could interview her on my radio show. She knew my work as an actor even though we never met, because we spent many of the same years working in and around Hollywood.

She was very receptive and said, "How about after the show tomorrow night?" I told her that we could set up our equipment in her dressing room, which she thought was the perfect place to do the interview. I'll never forget how gracious and professional she was when we recorded the show, even after giving an energetic and emotional performance to a standing ovation.

Francis began her career at the age of four singing and playing the accordion while attending church gatherings, family parties and Veterans hospitals. At the age of ten, she made her first television appearance on *Arthur Godfrey Talent Scouts*.

By the time she turned twelve, Connie was signed to sing on the variety show, *Star Time*, in which she appeared every week for four years. The producer of the show, George Shack, became her manager and convinced her to sign a recording contract with MGM records. Connie's first nine records didn't do very well, but her next record was a huge hit all over the world, entitled, "Who's Sorry Now?" thanks to *American Bandstand* host and her idol, Dick Clark.

Francis went on to record and become the top female recording artist in America and Europe. Her worldwide releases have been made available in the native languages of Italy, Germany, Japan, France, Spain and Portugal. On occasion, Swedish, Dutch or Greek vocals were added for good measure.

Her singing popularity led to her motion picture debut in *Where the Boys Are* in 1960. It became one of the top ten teen films of all time and the title song topped the charts in 15 countries. The song and movie gave her headline status at the Copacabana, Carnegie Hall, London's Palladium, Las Vegas' Sahara Hotel, Miami's Eden Roc, Lake Tahoe's Harrrah's, Hollywood's Coconut Grove, The Olympia Theater in Paris, and other famous venues throughout the world.

In addition to her own ABC television special, Connie appeared regularly on the *Ed Sullivan Show, Jack Benny, Dean Martin, Perry Como, Andy Williams, The Tonight Show,* plus many others. *The Exhibitor,* a motion picture magazine, awarded Connie the Laurel Award as Best Newcomer to Motion Pictures, and in the same year *PHOTOPLAY* magazine declared her Best Female Vocalist of the Year and bestowed upon her its first Gold Medal Award.

In 1974, Connie Francis's spectacular career was brought to a screeching halt when, after a performance at the Westbury Music Fair in Long Island, New York, she was brutally raped, beaten and robbed at knife point. This horrible ordeal led to a series of personal tragedies that, according to Connie, "No Hollywood writer could dream up, because it would be too impossible to believe."

For the next three years, Connie was unable to face the public and became reclusive and depressed, confining herself to the bedroom of her New Jersey mansion. In 1977, Connie underwent nasal surgery to correct a condition that precluded her from singing in air-conditioned venues and as a result of that surgery, she was unable to sing for an additional four years. "When I went to the recording studio for my first session after the operation, my blood just turned to ice. I knew my career was over. I believed I would never sing again."

In 1981, tragedy struck again with the gangland-style slaying of Connie's beloved brother, Georgie. "I can discuss just about anything that has occurred in my life, but not my brother's death," said Connie. That same year, however, after three subsequent surgical procedures, Connie learned that she could sing again.

Her triumphant return to the stage in the early 1980s was interrupted by a series of commitments to mental institutions, where Connie was diagnosed with manic-depression. With the help of medication and the loyalty and support of her family, friends and fans, Connie's illness was brought under control and she once again performed to sold-out houses throughout the country.

Connie Francis is the only recording artist to have been awarded ten golden discs for ten individual titles within a two-year period. It places her firmly in the top ten of the world's all-time gold disc winners. Her record sales are in excess of one hundred million copies.

Connie's most rewarding experiences have been her charitable activities. She was the 1969 Chairman of the Overseas Combined Charities which included CARE, UNICEF and USO. While North America was involved in Vietnam, Connie sang for the troops, receiving a welcome she will never forget, and still calls the trip, "The most memorable professional event of my life."

At the close of our interview, she reflected on the spectacular success of her career, as well as the devastating tragedies of her personal life. "I would like to be known for the heights I have reached, but also for the depths from which I have risen."

Connie Francis will forever remain at the peak of her life and career to me.

Shecky Greene
Comedian – Entertainer – Singer
Interviewed: 1996

I FIRST MET SHECKY GREENE, one of the greatest classic comedians and entertainers of all time, in a celebrity softball league in Hollywood, California in the early 1960s. Shecky was actually a pretty good athlete; a left-handed hitter and had decent running speed. He wasn't always available during the summer months when we played our games because he was busy working. But when Shecky could participate, he played well.

A couple of decades later we both became part of the show business Lunch Bunch at the Café Roma Restaurant in Beverly Hills, California, and became friends. I'm proud to say we've been friends ever since. Shecky was always fun to be with, sharing his countless jokes over the years. It was his gift of laughter and as Clint Eastwood said, it always "made my day." Although Chicago was the city where he was born and raised, it was Las Vegas, Nevada, where Shecky eventually felt at home on and off the stage.

Shecky loved to sing. I asked him when he first started. "I sang very well. I entertained people when I was 8 or 9 years old. I had a voice and did amateur productions in school. What's strange about that is that when I was really capable of singing, you know I really didn't have, as I got older, I really didn't have that strength of character and confidence to really do that."

Funny where life takes you because, for more than thirty years, Shecky Greene reigned as one of the most sought-after performers at all the major casinos in Las Vegas. Very few entertainers can make that distinction. It was not just his comedic talent that sustained him over the years, but his impersonations of well-known personalities, using his terrific singing voice, as well.

Shecky revealed, "When I was really on the road to success, I was making money and everything else in my twenties. I really started to climb. From Reno, I went to Las Vegas and that was the making of me." He expressed, "Elvis was my opening act in 1956 at the Frontier Hotel. And I never enjoyed and liked a kid as much as I did him."

Greene's ability to improvise is truly something to observe and enjoy. He never repeated the same routine, it was always different and always entertaining. I marveled at Shecky's intelligence, his observation of people and his photogenic memory that he combined with current events, transforming them into a humorous experience. He was sensitive, and had to be well-read to perform such successful routines the way he did.

It was during his rising career when Uncle Sam called and Shecky opted to join the Navy, serving over two years before being discharged. "I joined the Navy and was still in the Navy when I graduated high school. If there was never a war, I don't think I would have graduated high school." Another great comedic performer, Jonathan Winters, happen to serve on the same ship and what an entertaining combination they must have made! "On the ship, Jonathan Winters was a Marine, a private first class, we had a Marine group that took care of the captains." It wasn't long after Greene was discharged, when he became one of the most successful and highest paid entertainers, performing at all the best clubs and casinos, wherever and whenever he wanted to. Shecky said, "You look back and they're wonderful, the people that I worked with."

Looking to expand his entertainment horizons, Shecky left the nightclub circuit to appear on episodic television, game shows, concerts, talk shows and motion pictures. He did several television pilots for Screen Gems Productions, Metro Goldwyn Mayer Studios, Ziv Productions and the ABC Network. Shecky was scheduled to be one of the stars in the television hit series *Combat*, but after a few episodes he left the show. Shecky explained, "I was working in Las Vegas too at the time and they weren't writing the shows fast enough for me to do both."

He later returned to entertaining in nightclubs and casinos for many years until one night he walked off the stage in Vancouver, B.C. due to panic attacks. "I couldn't control it anymore. It was a genetic thing." He didn't perform for eight years and only returned periodically after that.

He and his wife Marie Musso, daughter of Vito Musso, the great tenor saxophone player, were residents of Palm Springs for many years. They later moved to the Las Vegas area. We miss seeing them, always having a few laughs whenever we spent time together. Knowing and loving Shecky and Marie, is all about laughter and friendship.

I once asked Shecky how he got his name, having been born as Sheldon. He said, "What's funny, my brother gave me that name. Everyone in the neighborhood had a nickname. I don't think we ever knew anyone's real name."

Shecky, your name is as special and unique as you are.

Anne Jeffreys
Actress – Singer
Interviewed: 1995

I MET ACTRESS, OPERA SINGER ANNE JEFFREYS at a charity tennis tournament hosted by actor Tommy Cook in Los Angeles, California. She was my partner in a mixed doubles match and we became friends from that day forward. We played in quite a number of celebrity tennis tournaments throughout the Los Angeles area, raising funds for many needy organizations and had so many fun times along the way. Anne loved tennis and was always trying to improve her game, along with an effervescent, competitive spirit, and was one of my favorite tennis doubles partners.

Anne Jeffreys began her stellar professional career as a teenage model for the John Roberts Powers Agency in New York City while studying for a career in opera. Anne reminisced, "At five, I sang my first tune in public and at ten I had my own radio show in Raleigh Durham, North Carolina. At fifteen, sixteen years old, my mother took me to New York to study and while I was studying somebody introduced us to JR Powers. I had a wonderful mother that was everything to me, anyway. I was raised by a single parent. She also managed my career."

Her operatic studies were interrupted when she accepted a role in the stage musical, *Fun for The Money*. The production was in Hollywood. Anne had to pay her Actor's Equity dues and had no income for weeks just after she and her mom sold everything to come to California. Her role in *Fun for the Money* led to her first movie role, *I Married an Angel* with Jeanette McDonnell and Nelson Eddy. "Nelson was wonderful. He nicknamed me the 'quiet one' because I was mesmerized when he came on in, *I Married an Angel*."

Shortly thereafter, she was put under contract to Republic Studios. She made twelve films for Republic, including a series of eight westerns with 'Wild Bill' Elliot and Gaby Hayes.

Anne remembered, "It was such a good school of learning in those days. If you cry real tears in a scene, that's not acting. You can convince an audience that you're really crying, but

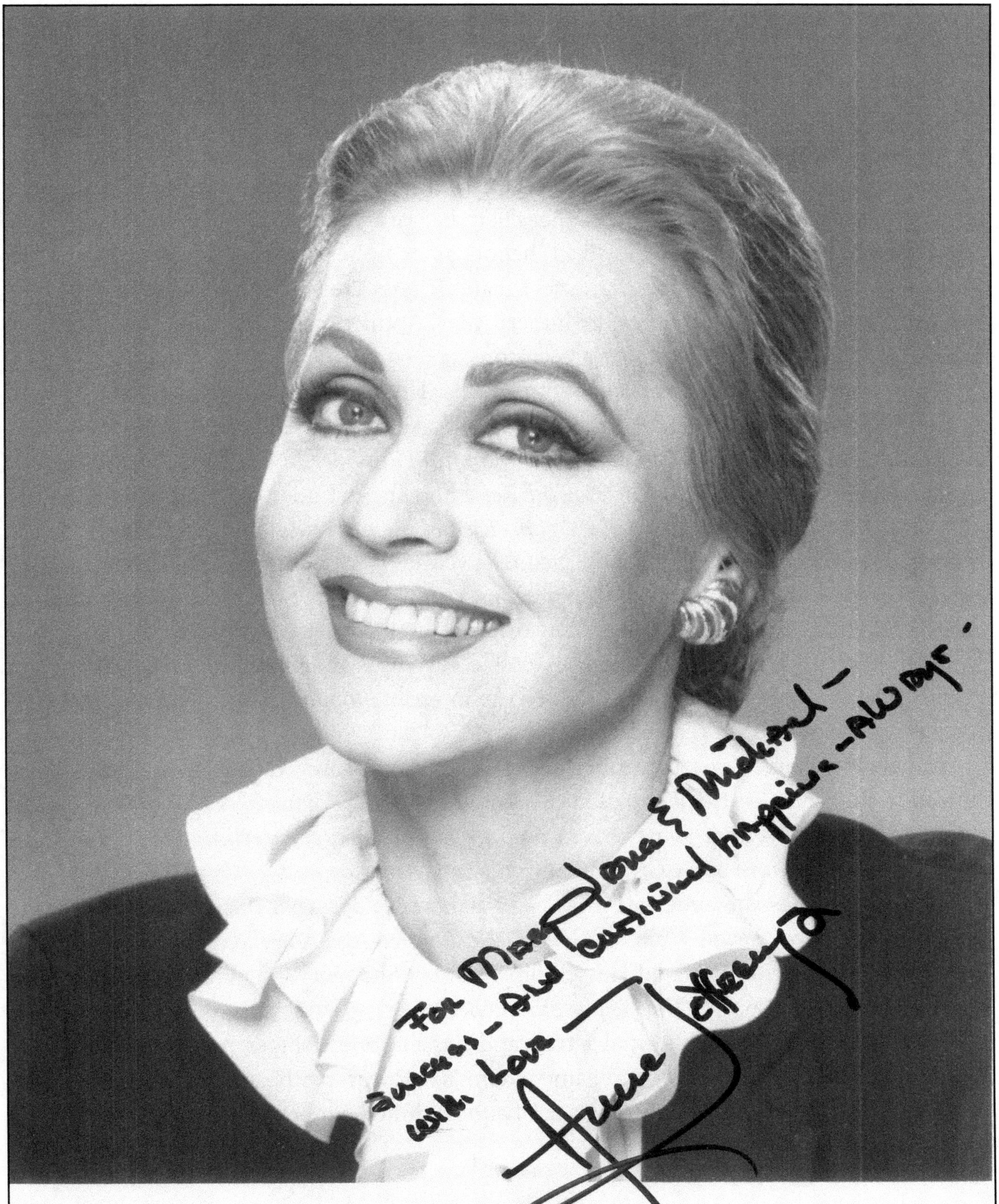
For Mary Jane & Michael —
success — and continued happiness — always.
with love —
Anne Jeffreys

you aren't really crying tears, then you're acting." Shortly thereafter, RKO Pictures bought out her contract, to co-star with Frank Sinatra in the motion picture, *Step Lively*.

Between her many film assignments at RKO, Anne continued her operatic studies and performed with the New York Symphony, The Ford Symphony and The Los Angeles Opera Company. She also performed for three seasons at the Greek Theater in Los Angeles, California, alternating with *Bittersweet* and *The Merry Widow*.

While there, Cole Porter offered her *Kiss Me Kate*. She spent two years and eight hundred and eighty-seven consecutive performances in that classic musical. During her *Kiss Me Kate* run at the Shubert Theater in New York, she met actor Robert Sterling, then starring in the *Gramercy Ghost* at the adjoining Morosco Theater. They were married six months after they met and were called The Romance of Shubert Alley. At the time of this interview, they were married forty-four years, with three grown sons.

Anne went on to star in a number of other films. They included *Boys Night Out, Dillinger, Riffraff, Dick Tracy, Nevada, Return of The Bad Man, Southern Double, Old Homestead, X Marks the Spot, Death Valley Manhunt, The Man from Thunder River, Sing Your Way Home, Genius at Work, Step-by-Step, Vacation in Reno* and the list goes on. Her stage plays are countless; *Kiss Me Kate, Destry Rides Again, Kismet, Bells Are Ringing, Camelot, Carousel, The Sound of Music*, performing in all the finest venues throughout the country.

Her highly successful club act led to the long-running and ever popular television series, *Topper*, delighting audiences all over the world.

Anne shared, "We went to the Sands Hotel in Las Vegas and played for six weeks and got a call from L.A. to work together in the television series, *Topper*, doing two years, seventy-nine episodes and now in reruns."

Anne guest-starred on numerous episodic television shows, variety shows, miniseries, movies of the week, and talk shows such as *Wagon Train, Bonanza, Steve Allen Show, Ed Sullivan Show, Milton Berle Show, Perry Como Show, Dr. Kildare, Joey Bishop Show, My Three Sons, The Tonight Show, Merv Griffin Show* and *Love American-Style*.

Television series she appeared in as a regular were *Love That Jill, The Delphi Bureau, Finder of Lost Loves*, seven years on *General Hospital* as Amanda Barrington, and on *Bay Watch*, playing the role of David Hasselhoff's mother. She received a Golden Globe award nomination for her work in *The Delphi Bureau Series*.

Anne Jeffreys, the quintessential actress and classical opera singer, combined her talents of singing and acting, played a good game of tennis and with her beauty and sophistication, was admired by all. She died in 2012 at age 94 and no doubt, her beautiful voice is serenading the angels.

Lainie Kazan
Actress – Entertainer
Interviewed: 2000

I met Lainie Kazan many years ago at a party of one of my very good friends, Norby Walters. She looked sensational and she still looks as lovely today. When I asked her to be a guest on my radio show, she immediately accepted. We made arrangements to do the show at the Friars' Club in Beverly Hills, California.

We sat comfortably in one of the booths and began our interview, very conversationally. Lainie brought a big smile, a lot of energy and fun to the show from the start. She began by saying, "I was, at the beginning of my career, a 'character' who sang. I always sang as part of my character. It took a lot for me to learn how to be me."

That's surprising to me because Lainie Kazan is a supremely talented singer, actress and recording artist who has virtually reached the pinnacle in every area of performance, even as Barbara Streisand's Broadway understudy in *Funny Girl*. Her career took off, given the opportunity to display her electrifying talent, appearing on all the top variety and celebrity talk shows, including twenty-six appearances on *The Dean Martin Show*. Lainie shared with me and our audience, "Through that relationship with Frank (Sinatra) and Dean (Martin), I really started to have this unbelievable visibility and career. That's really where it began." She went on to host her own variety special for NBC, as well as performing at some of the finest nightclubs in the country. She was a frequent headliner in the famed Oak Room at the Algonquin Hotel in New York City.

Her motion picture career began when director Francis Ford Coppola watched her perform at San Francisco's Fairmont Hotel. He offered her a plum role in his film, *One from The Heart*.

Lainie went on to appear in many other films including, *My Favorite Year,* for which she received a Golden Globe nomination for her fine performance. About working on *My Favorite Year,* "I worked with Peter O'Toole; an unbelievable experience. What an

extraordinary gentleman and what a learning experience it was for me. Richard Benjamin was an amazing director. It was a joyous set, it was so congenial, the easiest, most wonderful experience." Lainie Kazan reprised her role in the Broadway musical version of *My Favorite Year*, winning a Tony award nomination for best actress. Her other films were, *Lust in The Dust, Delta Force, Beaches, Harry and The Hendersons, The Cemetery Club, The Big Hit, The Crew,* and *What's Cooking?*

Some of Kazan's episodic television appearances include an Emmy award nomination for her performance in *St. Elsewhere* and an Ace nomination for *The Paper Chase*. Lainie confided, "After I had turned down a lot of roles, to break a stereotype, I figured I better take one of these jobs. I just wanted to play a woman with feelings and passions. That led me to my role in *Paper Chase*, that got me an Ace nomination."

Her recurring television roles were in *The Nanny, Veronica's Closet, Touched by an Angel,* and a children's special for The Wonderful World of Disney entitled, *Safety Patrol*. Several years after our interview, Lainie played one of her most memorable roles, as the mom in *My Big Fat Greek Wedding* and *My Big Fat Greek Wedding 2*. Lainie's earthy quality made her absolutely perfect for those two performances.

Her nightclub engagements included sold-out performances at The Cinegrill and The Catalina Bar and Grill in Los Angeles, Trump's Castle and Harrah's Casino in Las Vegas and Atlantic City. Lainie Kazan and her daughter, Jennifer Bona, sang on Lainie's new CD, *Body and Soul*, a collection of graceful, feline-like sentiment, that smolders with what Rex Reed remarked about Lainie, "More talent in her little finger than most singers have in their dreams." Lainie remarked, "My album, *Body and Soul*, it was a labor of love, produced by Tony Bennet's son, Dave Bennett. My favorite ballads are on it. It's a wonderful CD that I'm very proud of." It was released on the Music Masters label and distributed by BMG Music and Distribution.

Kazan's career was put on hold for a while in the 1990s. "After my big success, I had an accident and was very sick. I was in a wheelchair for a couple of years and my career took a huge slump. The Playboy Club brought me back and made my life more interesting."

Lainie Kazan has been a supporter of numerous charities. She received the Woman of the Year award from the B'nai B'rith organization, and has graced the stage for many AIDS benefits, telethons and nonprofits throughout the United States. She serves on the board for the Young Musicians Foundation, AIDS Project LA and B'nai B'rith. In 1990, she was presented with the Israeli Peace Award.

This talented artist will continue to delight audiences, with the versatility she embraced throughout her multi-faceted career. We look forward to much more film, stage and recording entertainment from Lainie Kazan in the years to come. Lanie did learn over the years "how to be me" through her talent on stage, with her songs and with laughter, that she readily shares with all of us.

23

Howard Keel
Singer – Actor
Interviewed: 1995

I met singer, actor Howard Keel in the Metro Goldwyn Mayer Studios Commissary, the first year I was under contract to the Studio in 1956. I was impressed with his sincere greeting, as he pointed to my picture on the wall. "Great shot," he commented. I returned the compliment by telling him I was a big fan of his work. We shook hands when he left and he wished me good luck during my stay at the studio. I saw Howard only a few times over the years, until we both became permanent residents in the Palm Springs, California area, years later.

We were both invited to many of the same celebrity golf tournaments every year, including the biggest event in our desert area, The Frank Sinatra Invitational. My wife Mary Jane and I became friends with Howard and his wife Judy, and remained friends until he passed away in 2004 at the age of 85. Howard and Judy both had a great sense of humor and we shared many laughs. Judy moved away from the desert to be closer to her family after Howard's passing.

Howard was the son of a coal miner in South Central, Illinois. His dad spent four years in the Navy, sailed around the world and came back to the coal mines. It was a rough time when his dad passed away in 1930 when Howard was eleven. "I got lucky when I was sixteen, I got out and came to California. I worked at Douglas Aircraft for eight years. Certain people touch you in your life and things put you in another direction entirely." He was put on the right path. "American Music Theater, I worked for them and studied very hard. I sang for a concert agency, NCAC, and then I sang for Rodgers and Hammerstein and it was the easiest audition I ever gave. I went to New York and saw my first musical. I auditioned and they signed me to a three-year contract."

Keel's stellar career started in the Broadway production of *Carousel* and shortly thereafter he starred in the long-running, hit musical *Oklahoma*. He then went to London's Drury Lane creating the same amorous cowboy, Curly MacLaine. "Opening night in London, it was an incredible, incredible night. The curtain calls lasted 45 minutes."

Two years later he signed a seven-year contract with MGM Studios and immediately starred in the Irving Berlin Musical, *Annie Get Your Gun*, opposite Betty Hutton. Howard shared, "Betty was a good gal. She was just so intense with what she was trying to do, you had to be on your p's and q's to keep up with her." The movie and Howard became a huge success. A long list of films and musicals followed: *Pagan Love Song, Showboat, Lovely to Look At, Kiss Me Kate* and he was on loan to Warner Bros. to star with Doris Day in *Calamity Jane*. Howard received rave reviews and the film won an Oscar for the best song entitled, "Secret Love." "It was very exciting. I couldn't quite believe what was happening to me." Two of Howard's greatest hits were *Seven Brides for Seven Brothers* and *Kismet* with good actors, good athletes and good acrobats. They were two of my favorite musicals.

Several films later, Howard returned to the stage in musicals, touring America, Canada, Great Britain and Australia. He was highly successful in the dramatic role of Franklin D. Roosevelt in the Tony Award-winning play, *Sunrise at Campobello*. Eventually, musicals became too expensive to produce, the musical productions which had been Keel's mainstay in Hollywood.

His life changed in 1981 when the executive producer of *Dallas* came along and cast Keel to play the second husband of Barbara Bell Geddes in the popular television series *Dallas*. He stayed with that production for the next ten years and in his own words, "Best job I ever had!"

As a singer, Howard Keel recorded on Warwick Records, "Silver Eagle" and "Telstar" and following, "Close to My Heart" was released on E.M.I. Records.

Howard told us about his vocal gift. "The voice is like an instrument, Michael. I've been blessed. I've been given a fine instrument and enough intelligence to use it and I just feel that I have to give it back. I love to sing and I love entertaining people." He added, "The problem with singing is the fact that you don't hear yourself the way people do."

Howard raised a great deal of money through charity, lending his name to the Howard Keel Golf Classic, an annual tournament benefiting the National Society of Prevention of Cruelty to Children.

In 2019, Howard Keel had one of the highest honors bestowed on him, as one who had contributed their talented share to the western genre in films and on television. His outstanding work, his contribution to the history of the West, will live on in perpetuity at the National Cowboy and Western Heritage Museum in Oklahoma City, Oklahoma. Howard received the award posthumously, and was most deserving of this honor.

Howard must be singing, dancing and riding his horse in Cowboy heaven.

Harmon Killebrew
Major League Baseball – Hall of Fame
Interviewed: 1999

I MET MAJOR LEAGUE BASEBALL HALL OF FAMER Harmon Killebrew when we were both rookies in spring training with the Washington Senators in Orlando, Florida in 1955. He was the top prospect to make the ball club that year because he had tremendous power. When I was fielding ground balls and he was hitting in the batting cage, my attention diverted to the sound of the crack of the bat as he squared off on the pitch. The ball looked like a rocket, flying over the fence. I knew then he was destined to become a Hall of Famer. We didn't hang out during spring training with so much to do, but we talked baseball whenever we could.

After I left baseball and became an actor, many years later I had the fortuitous opportunity to play in Harmon's celebrity charity golf tournament for ten years in Phoenix and Scottsdale, Arizona. Hall of Famers from almost every sport and a few lucky actors that had played professionally, like myself, gathered each year to raise funds for several of Harmon's favorite charities. It was always successful and fun, with a family feeling. Harmon and I were very close friends until the time he passed away at the age of 74, in 2011.

Harmon Killebrew was born in Payette, Idaho. Starting at age 18, Harmon shared, "I really didn't have any idea of signing a major league contract at that time. That's what I eventually wanted to do, but in those days, they weren't giving scholarships to play baseball." Harmon continued, "Senator Welker kept telling Clark Griffith about this young kid in Idaho that could help him win some ball games. Ossie Bluege, farm director of the team at that time, came to Idaho to see me and said, 'Hey, I think we should try to sign this kid.'" That day Harmon hit a 435-foot homerun and that night Ossie Bluege called Mr. Griffith. "I signed a three-year, major league contract with the Washington Senators. Under the old rules, I went directly to the major leagues in 1954." He got some excellent advice about how he could improve his game. "Ralph Kiner talked to me when I was 18."

He said, 'If you'll just move up on the plate a little more, you'll probably hit more home runs. I tried it and it worked pretty well for me.'" Boy, did it ever! Harmon told us, "My first regular season was in 1959. It took me nearly five years until I could break into the lineup in the major leagues."

Killebrew went on to play twenty-two years in the major leagues, twenty-one with the Washington Senators and Minnesota Twins combined, and finished his final year in 1975 with the Kansas City Royals. Harmon recalled, "I played my first major league game in 1955 at Connie Mack Stadium in Philadelphia. I played my first couple of games in the major leagues at second base." Killebrew became the fifth leading home run hitter of all time with 573 home runs, led the American League in home runs six times and compiled 1,584 runs batted in. Killebrew made the American League All-Star Team thirteen times and played three different positions, played on the World Series winning team in 1965, American League Most Valuable Player and Player of the Year in 1969, Player of the Year and The Lou Gehrig Award in 1970, Idaho Sports Hall of Fame in 1979, Babe Ruth Sultan of Swat Award in 1964, 1969 and 1988. Killebrew was inducted into the Major League Baseball Hall of Fame in Cooperstown, New York in 1984. He was also inducted into Ted William's Hitters Hall of Fame in 1996 and made the All-Century Team in 1999.

He began his second career while still an active player with WTCN Television of Minneapolis, where he hosted *The Harmon Killebrew Pregame Show* from 1961 to 1972. He continued after retiring in 1975, broadcasting again for WTCN of Minneapolis for the Minnesota Twins Baseball Club from 1976 through 1978. He then moved to KPIX television where he broadcasted for the Oakland A's baseball club in 1979 through 1982. In 1983, he was broadcaster for the California Angels and returned to the Twin Cities in 1984, broadcasting radio and television for the Minnesota Twins through 1988. Harmon said, "It was exciting. If I couldn't be on the field playing, broadcasting in the booth was the next best thing to it." Killebrew established his own business of professional endorsements through which he made many appearances and was also devoted to giving back to others.

He founded the Danny Thompson Memorial Golf Tournament, in Sun Valley, Idaho in 1977 and served on the board actively until 1987. The tournament contributed more than $2 million to Leukemia research since its inception. Since 1991, Harmon served as the national spokesperson for The World Children's Baseball Fair and represented them in both the United States and Japan. He served on the Board of Directors since 1992. Killebrew helped to establish and attend the Harmon Killebrew Signature Classic Golf Tournament in Lincoln, Nebraska from 1996 to 1997. In November 1997, he sponsored the Inaugural Annual Harmon Killebrew Invitational Golf Tournament, benefiting The Vista Hospice Care Foundation in Scottsdale, Arizona.

In 1998, Harmon and his wife, Nita, founded the Harmon Killebrew Foundation, Ltd. to aid worthy charities such as The Baseball Assistance Team, Diva House, the country's first pediatric hospice, Vista Hospice Care Foundation and The World's Children's Baseball Fair.

A very meaningful occurrence happened to us in the 1990s. Mary Jane and I were invited to a special dinner and golf tournament in Las Vegas, Nevada commemorating the late, legendary baseball Hall of Famer, Mickey Mantle. Mickey's family was there along with other distinguished guests, including Harmon. Harmon Killebrew was one of the baseball players on the classic original *Home Run Derby* television show in 1959-1960, of which Mary Jane's dad was the host. Reuniting with Harmon was meant to be, for both of us.

I'd like to share that Harmon had the most beautiful handwriting of anyone I ever knew. When he signed his baseballs, it was like it was stamped on the ball. Once, I mentioned how beautiful and perfect his penmanship was, and he gave me a little chuckle and said, "Michael, I know."

Having an opportunity to get to know Harmon again, and play ten years in his golf tournament to help him support the charities that were dear to him, is something I'll always be grateful for. A man with tremendous Hall of Fame power, on and off the baseball field, is the way I'll always remember my friend, Harmon Killebrew.

Ralph Kiner
Major League Baseball – Hall of Fame
Interviewed: 1995

I MET MAJOR LEAGUE BASEBALL HALL OF FAMER Ralph Kiner many years ago at the Frank Sinatra Invitational in Palm Springs, California. Ralph was a long-time resident of the desert area in the off-season from baseball. He was a very good golfer and was invited to all the celebrity charity tournaments throughout the Valley. I was invited to the same golf tournaments as Ralph, so we got to see each other quite a lot during the years. We socialized often and became very good friends with he and his wife, Diann and his three children by his first wife, Nancy Chaffee Kiner. Nancy was a celebrity in her own right, she was the indoor ladies' singles and women's doubles tennis champion, three consecutive times. And, of course, she became a household name thanks to her Chapstick commercials. As time went by, we watched his three youngsters grow up to be fine adults, Scott, Michael and daughter, Tracey.

Ralph Kiner was born in New Mexico and is the only Baseball Hall of Famer from the state. He grew up in Alhambra, California playing baseball on semi-pro teams when he was 12 years old. Ralph shared his truth about baseball, "You can't learn baseball, unless you play it."

Kiner played 10 years in the major leagues with three different ball clubs, mostly with the Pittsburgh Pirates for seven-and-a-half years. Ralph shared, "I had a great situation with the Pirates." He then went with the Chicago Cubs and finished his stellar career with the Cleveland Indians. He added, "I was happy about being traded to Chicago, they only played day ball in Chicago and I love the city of Chicago. Great park to play in and great fans. In Cleveland, the best manager I ever played for was Al Lopez, an ex-major league catcher who became the manager of the Cleveland Indians."

Kiner hit 369 home runs in those ten years, led the National League in home runs for seven consecutive years from 1946 through 1952. He remembered, "I led the league in home runs and didn't want to take a 25% cut. Mr. Rickey said, 'Son, where did we finish?' I said,

'last' and he said, 'We can finish last without you.' So, I took the 25% cut; I got the message. I wasn't gonna play unless I signed." Ralph batted in over 100 runs, six times, with a lifetime batting average of 279, had a total of 1,015 runs batted in, voted to the All-Star Team six times and is second only to the great Babe Ruth, hitting home runs per time at bat. During these years, with all of his successes, Ralph noted that in 1947, the business of baseball was changing, "It was basically a union and two things they were fighting for; a minimum salary and the other thing was a pension plan."

He hit over 50 home runs twice in his career, 51 home runs in 1947, tying with Johnny Mize, a left-handed hitter, first baseman for the Giants and 54 home runs in 1949. Ralph said, "Baseball great, Hank Greenberg was all business and he told me that you gotta have a professional attitude and every time you go to the plate you gotta have a desire and you have to have a plan. He really installed that into my thinking."

In 1949, Kiner led the National League with 54 home runs, knocked in 127 runs and hit for a 310-batting average. What an outstanding year he had and he didn't win The Most Valuable Player Award that year. In my opinion, that's hard to believe. But Ralph explained, "The object of baseball is to win the baseball game, no matter what the personal achievements are. The most frustrating thing you can have happen to you in baseball is play with bad ballclubs because you can say you hit three homeruns in a ballgame and drove in six or seven runs and still not win. It's pretty hard to win."

Upon his retirement, Kiner entered the broadcast booth for the Chicago White Sox in 1961. The following year he became the announcer and also hosted a post-game show, "Kiner's Korner" for the New York Mets, until he retired 52 years later, in 2013.

Ralph Kiner was inducted into The Major League Baseball Hall of Fame in Cooperstown, New York in 1975, with one regret, "I never had a chance to play in a World Series."

Ralph was elected into the New York Mets Hall of Fame in 1984 and in 1987, the Pittsburgh Pirates retired his uniform, Number 4, at Forbes Field. The New York Mets organization honored him on Ralph Kiner Night at Shea Stadium on July 14, 2007. Kiner retired from broadcasting in 2013 and in 2014 he passed away at the age of 91 with his family at his side, in Rancho Mirage, California.

My wife and I will never forget that Ralph introduced us to sweet potato fries. When visiting New York, he invited us to watch a New York Mets game in his suite at Shea Stadium. They served food in the suite and on the menu were sweet potato fries. We tried them and we were hooked! We'll always thank Ralph for introducing us to one of our favorite side dishes. Sweet potato fries are quite a leap from all his accomplishments in baseball, but for us, it's another wonderful memory to recall.

Morgana King
Actress — Singer
Interviewed: 2007

I FIRST MET ACTRESS, SINGER AND RECORDING ARTIST Morgana King at a social event in Los Angeles, California, introduced by our mutual friend, actor Harry Guardino. Morgana and I instantly shared how much we appreciated each other's work in show business. Our relationship grew over the years and we became close friends, until she passed away in 2018, at the age of 87.

Morgana had a home in Palm Springs, California next door to Jilly Rizzo, Frank Sinatra's best friend, long before we moved to the desert. She was working and traveling throughout the country, when my radio talk show got underway in Palm Springs. I asked her to be a guest on the show and she immediately accepted.

About her early years, Morgana shared, "My sister and I worked in a legitimate theater, the Shubert Theater. I sat on the steps during a performance and said, 'Oooo, this is where I'm going, and I started concentrating on drama.' She revealed about her singing career, "I worked all the joints in New York when I was sixteen. I opened every single club he ever owned on the East side, Mr. Frank Costello. He heard me singing in The Place, this is 1946. He was the guiding light for me." Costello changed her name from Morgan to Morgana, and thus Morgana King was born.

King performed in virtually every New York club. They included The Village Vanguard, Birdland, The Versailles, Basin Street East, Basin Street West, The Bon Soir, where she worked for one week and they kept her on for twelve weeks, The Red Carpet, The Beau Brummel, Jillys, The RSVP Club and so many more.

She also performed in well-known, out-of-town clubs like The Celebrity Room and Celebrity Club in Philadelphia, Detroit's Flame Club, The Pirates Den in Bermuda, Miami's Eden Roc, Chicago's Cloister and Mr. Kelly's.

Morgana knew and worked with so many great, talented people throughout her singing and acting career. She especially remembered, "Lady Billy Holiday, whom I adored. I went

to see her at The Strand Theater in New York with (Count) Basie's Band. Dressed all in white against her skin color, she was gorgeous." King appeared in concerts at Carnegie Hall, Town Hall, Jazz Under the Stars in Central Park and The Hollywood Bowl. She recorded on Mercury Records, Mainstream, RCA Camden, United Artists, Reprise, Paramount, Muse, and Sony labels. Her great rendition of "A Taste of Honey" earned her a gold record. "My husband produced 'Taste of Honey' which they never gave him credit for." She had giants in the business helping her, including the likes of Frank Sinatra, Jilly Rizzo and her husband. Morgana said that, "I was like that picture inside the frame," referring to all the wonderful support she got with the song.

Speaking of Sinatra, Morgana said that she went way back with the Sinatra family, "Mr. Sinatra's father was related to my family in Catania, Sicily. My mother and father were from Sicily. We were paisans." Continuing about Sinatra, "He was the greatest musician, actor I've known in my whole life. When he opened his mouth, who sang like that?"

Morgana made numerous guest appearances on all the top television and variety shows: *The Dean Martin Show, Danny Kaye Show, The Andy Williams Show, Mike Douglas Show, Johnny Carson Show, Dinah Shore Show, The Hollywood Palace* and *The Merv Griffin Show*.

She toured extensively in South America with the Buddy Rich Band in São Paulo, Brazil at the Teatro Recordo Concert and a number of television programs in São Paulo and Rio de Janeiro.

Morgana's career expanded into motion pictures and television. She did a memorable role, playing Mama Corleone in *The Godfather and Godfather II*. She also appeared in other films such as *Nunzio, Winter Roses* and *A Brooklyn State of Mind*.

Her television shows included, *Jigsaw John, Mr. President, Obsessed to Kill* and *Deadly Intentions* with Cloris Leachman. *NBC* magazine did a show with her entitled, *Morgana King Documentary* with David Brinkley.

Morgana was a woman for all seasons, and through it all she shared her life through her talents of singing and acting. It must have been an honor for Morgana to have been chosen to work in the first two *Godfather* films as the wife of Marlon Brando. Hollywood gave her an opportunity and made her an offer she couldn't refuse. King told us that she absolutely loved working with Marlon Brando and Al Pacino.

Morgana wisely said, "Nobody really goes when you leave history, you're always there." And she added, "The wonderful thing about my life is that people respected my art."

Frankie Laine
Entertainer
Interviewed: 2003

I MET INTERNATIONAL SINGING, ACTOR and recording artist Frankie Laine at his beautiful home in Southern California in 2003. It was designed by his late wife Nan Gray, a former Universal Studios starlet, whom he married in 1950. Nan designed the house that sits high atop a sandstone cliff in the Point Loma area of San Diego, California. From that vantage point, he had a panoramic view of the harbor, the Coronado Islands and the Baja Peninsula in nearby Mexico. Over the years, their hobbies included horseback riding, coin collecting, golfing and painting. They both loved boating, and at one time spent many happy hours fishing for Marlin and Sailfish on a yacht they built and christened the good ship *My Desire*. It was named after his massive hit recording of "That's My Desire," a song that burst onto the scene like musical fireworks in 1947, with praise that poured in from all corners, from young and old alike, for this gifted and versatile artist. Frankie Laine possessed a tall, handsome, charismatic presence to accompany his distinctive, unique singing style. Shortly after we met, we made arrangements to record his radio show interview at his home.

Laine was the holder of twenty-one gold records. Only a handful of performers have demonstrated the lasting appeal it takes to sustain the onslaught of fads and changing trends over the years and he was the classic example. His impeccable musicianship kept him an International favorite for decades. Frankie shared the beginning of his singing career. "I started doing a song that I had learned in Cleveland from a young girl called, 'That's My Desire,' which was really an old song but I introduced it as a new song for me. Then I recorded it and it broke everything open."

After the song made it big, he continued to record exciting new material, while maintaining a healthy respect for the songs like "Mule Train," "That Lucky Old Sun," "I Believe," "Jezebel," "Rocking Chair" and "You Gave Me a Mountain," written especially for him by his good friend and recording artist, Marty Robbins. Frankie talked about Marty and working in Las Vegas. "We never worked together. I only got to see him once on stage

in Vegas." About working in Las Vegas at venues like the Desert Inn, Landmark, Riviera and at the Frontier, Frankie shared, "I had twenty-five years in Vegas. I used to stay a month to six weeks." At that time, for an entertainer to have that long length of engagements in Las Vegas, was exceptional.

Many of Laine's most popular tunes were assembled into an album entitled, *The World of Frankie Laine*, that topped the charts in England in 1982. Since then, that LP has been issued in forty-three different countries. "It had a long life. I had no idea that this album was going to do what it's done," Frankie said.

Laine appeared as an actor in several motion pictures and numerous television and radio shows. He also had his own television variety show in the mid-1950s. He became the first and the most successful of the singers to be identified with title songs. He performed title songs for seven motion pictures, including, *Blowing Wild* for Warner Bros., *Blazing Saddles* for Mel Brooks and his featured recording of the successful television series, *Rawhide*, which is one of the most popular TV theme songs of all time. "I remember they called me in to see an episode to see if I wanted to do the song. That's what made me do it, seeing all those steers!" Frankie added, "I guess the song was partially responsible for the success of the show."

In 1996, Laine was presented with a Lifetime Achievement Award at the 27th Annual Songwriters Hall of Fame Award ceremony at the New York Sheraton Hotel. It was his first New York appearance in more than twenty years and he gave a performance to remember, singing, "Cry of The Wild Goose," "That's My Desire," "We'll Be Together Again," which he co-wrote with Carl Fisher.

"I met Carl Fisher and Carl turned out to be a wonderful man and a great musician and if it wasn't for him, I might not be sitting here doing this interview with you. Carl and I began to write together and he was looking for a lyric writer. Our first song together was 'We'll be Together Again.'" Frankie finished the Award Show with the dramatic song, "Jezebel," which brought the audience to its feet, several times.

Laine skyrocketed to the top after a seventeen-year wait. He went up from there and had a stellar career, known throughout the world as an incredibly talented musician, singer, songwriter, actor and a world class entertainer. As our interview progressed, I knew I was in the presence of a gifted, musical genius and a man who loved his life and the many gifts he was given, gifts he shared with all of us. Frankie passed away in 2007 at age 93, but his music will continue to live on.

Looking back on his career throughout our interview, Frankie shared his thoughts, expressing them with a touch of nostalgia, "I think sometimes of those early days; a wonderful feeling."

28

Tommy Lasorda
Major League Baseball – Hall of Fame
Interviewed: 1999

I met Tommy Lasorda when he was the coach for the Los Angeles Dodgers and during the second year the Dodgers played at the Los Angeles Memorial Coliseum in 1959. I met him at the same time I met Al Campanis, who was Vice President of Player Personnel. Because I was a former professional ballplayer, we all got acquainted in a very short period of time and became friends.

At the time, I was in the middle of filming the movie *Seven Thieves* at 20th Century Fox Studios in Los Angeles. I told Tommy and Al about the stars I was working with: Edward G. Robinson, Rod Steiger, Joan Collins and famous director Henry Hathaway. They were both big fans of Robinson's work. I invited them to be my guests at the Studio to meet Eddie and the rest of the cast, and to have lunch afterwards at the studio commissary. It was the first time for both men visiting a movie set. They were curious and full of questions about filming scenes and moviemaking, and were so impressed with all the coordinating talent surrounding the actors. Al made an astute on-the-spot comparison, "The director is much like a manager of a ballclub, who depends on his coaches to put it all together with him."

From that day on, I had an open invitation to any Dodger game. Consequently, I spent many years at the ballpark sitting with Campanis in his private box and enjoyed countless conversations about baseball with one of the finest minds in the game. In the early days, one could visit the clubhouse before and after the game, and I had the occasional opportunity for candid conversations with Lasorda. Later on, the league disallowed visits like that except for business or special occasions. Tom and Al were a pleasure to be with, always willing to share the nuances of the great American pastime. They had a great friendship, with respect and love for one another, as well.

Tommy Lasorda was born in Norristown, Pennsylvania and always spoke lovingly about his family, especially his father. "My father stood at the head of the table and told me and my

four brothers, 'You five guys are lucky. You're born in the greatest country in the world, the land of opportunity. You can be anything you wanna be in this country. Love your country, do everything you can to keep this country the best.'" Continuing this train of thought, he added, 'He embedded this patriotism that's been with me my entire life. He taught us respect, which carried us through life.'" With those values, he developed his focus around his love of baseball. "Self-confidence, without a doubt, is the first step to success," Tommy said. "I love baseball. I didn't want anything but baseball. I played baseball all day long and there wasn't nothing in this world that meant more to me than baseball."

Tommy is regarded by many as the greatest ambassador in the history of major league baseball. He spent more than fifty years in professional baseball, pitched sixteen years in the minor leagues, three years in the majors, managed eight years in the minors plus winning five pennants. His teams never finished lower than third place and Tommy spent four years on Walter Alston's coaching staff. He then managed the Los Angeles Dodgers for twenty years before his retirement in 1996.

During those years, his Dodger teams won 1,558 games while losing 1,404, compiling a .526 percentage, placing him 24th on the all-time list for managers with over 1,000 wins. Tommy guided his team to two Worlds Championships, four National League pennants and has been atop the Western Division eight different seasons. After he retired, Lasorda was named Vice President of the Los Angeles Dodgers and shortly thereafter was named interim General Manager, assuming all player personnel responsibilities. He relinquished those duties when he was promoted to Senior Vice President in 1998. His job consisted of scouting, evaluating and teaching minor league players, as well as spreading baseball goodwill to people all over the world.

Tommy won numerous awards throughout his outstanding career, to name only a few: Minor League Manager of the Year by *The Sporting News* in 1970, Manager of the Year by United Press International and Associated Press in 1977, Manager of the Year by Associated Press in 1981, National League Manager of the Year by Baseball America and Co-Manager of the Year by *The Sporting News* in 1988.

In addition, Lasorda was the recipient of the Association of Professional Baseball Players of America's Inaugural Milton Richman Memorial Award with Sparky Anderson in 1987, The Baseball Writers Association Philadelphia Chapters Humanitarian Award in 1993, Los Angeles Junior Chamber of Commerce Award of Merit in 1997, Touchdown Club of Columbus' Baseball Ambassador of the Year in 1997, Arete's Courage in Sports Award in 1997 and was honored by the President of the Dominican Republic in 1997 for his dedication to the game of baseball throughout his career.

Tommy is also a champion off the baseball diamond. He was a former spokesperson for the American Heart Association and has received an honorary doctorate degree from Pepperdine University, St. Thomas University and the University of Phoenix.

It is my opinion Tom Lasorda was one of the greatest managers who ever managed in the big leagues, because he had the innate ability to get the most out of his players. He made them believe that they were a lot better than they thought they were. He was a cheerleader, a role model and a father figure to all who knew, respected and worked with him. He said in our interview, "My belief was I always tried to run a team, an organization, like family. We're gonna spend more time together than with our own families. We want to be close; we want to be family."

Tommy was inducted into the National Baseball Hall of Fame in Cooperstown, New York in 1997. Sharing his thoughts, from that wonderful day, "In Cooperstown, being inducted into the Hall of Fame, I'm living a dream and I'm the happiest guy in the world. I just want the Dodgers to become the best team in baseball." Tommy Lasorda was National Baseball's oldest living Hall of Famer at age 93, before he left us in January 2021. Rest in Peace my friend.

Rod Laver

Association of Tennis Professionals — Tennis Hall of Fame

Interviewed: 1998

I HAD THE PLEASURE OF MEETING TENNIS great Rod 'The Rocket' Laver many years ago in Myrtle Beach, South Carolina, where he and fellow tennis great, Roy Emerson had a tennis camp. Rod invited two other outstanding Australian tennis champions, Ken Rosewall and John Newcombe, plus several Hollywood celebrities as invited guests to play with the students and patrons of the event. It was an enjoyable weekend that started on Friday and finished on Monday, playing on Har-Tru surfaces; a green hard clay court surface.

Even though it was very hot and humid, we had a lot of fun playing with different partners and even lost a few pounds from the humidity over the weekend and so did the four Aussies. All in all, they were hospitable hosts and we were all fortunate to watch four of the greatest tennis players of all time in action. They played several doubles exhibition matches and it was, without a doubt, the most enjoyable tennis matches I've ever watched.

During our radio interview, Rod shared two things that he believed were true concerning tennis players. "The magic height for a tennis player is six feet, six-feet-two. And, you can smother your voice on the hit of the ball, when you hit the ball. That's what I call timing." Rod was so knowledgeable about every nuance of the game.

Laver and Emerson had another tennis camp in California that I was invited to, as well. Tennis was a very popular sport then and all age groups benefitted by being taught by two of the greatest players to ever play the game. Rod liked grass courts the best. "A good grass court was, I think, most all the players would say, there's nothing better to play on."

As the years rolled by, I ran into Rod in one of the suites at the ATP tennis matches that take place each year at The Indian Wells Tennis Gardens in Southern California, and he was always friendly.

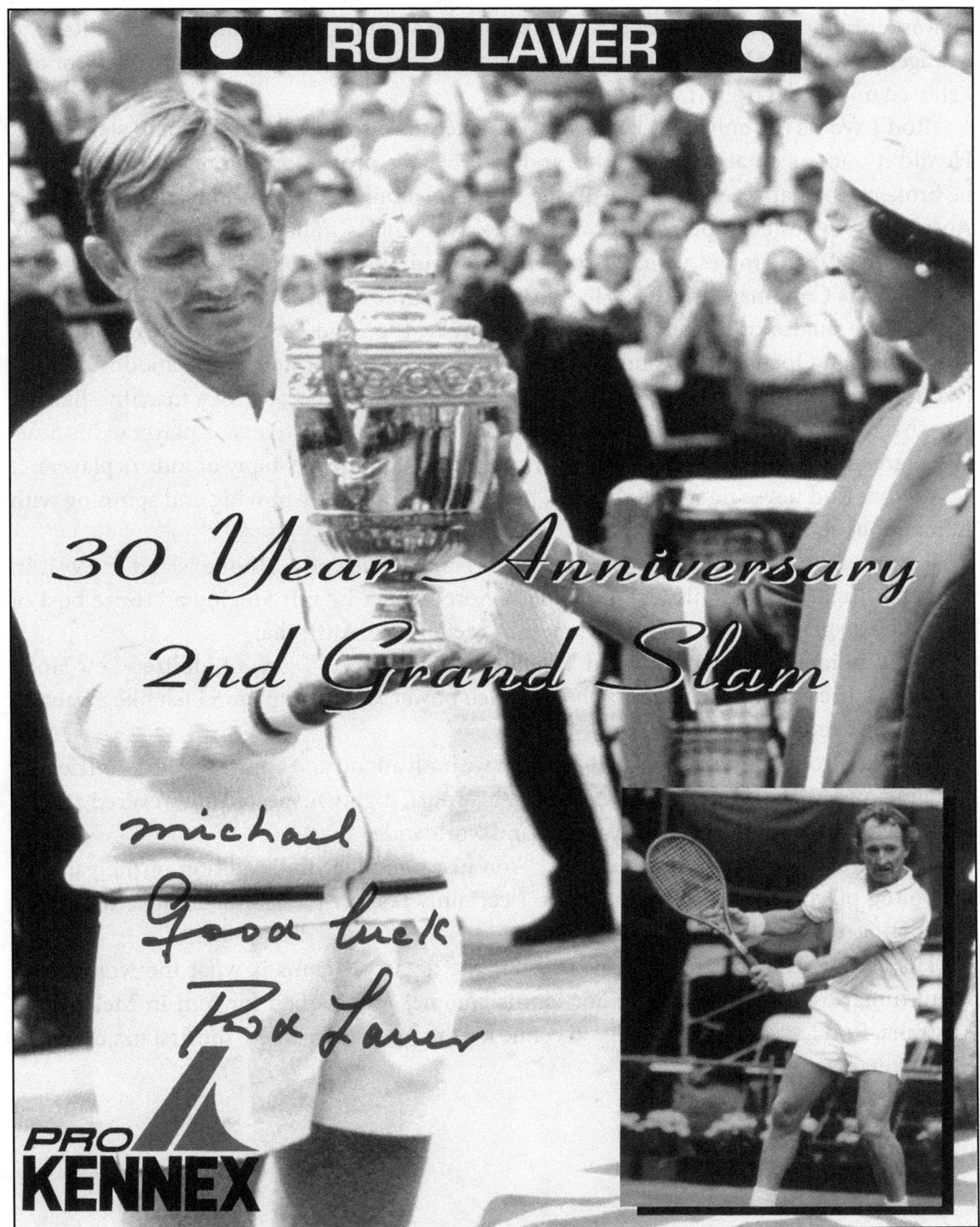

We would chat and catch up on what was going on in our lives. I interviewed Rod when he was a resident and professional tennis pro at the Morningside Country Club, in Rancho Mirage, California. He shared, "I felt very fortunate that a lot of things fell into place for me. I started out on the right track."

Rod Laver is the only player in professional tennis history to win the grand slam twice. He did it once as an amateur in 1962 and in 1969 as a professional, a record not likely to be broken. The native Australian won the singles championship at Wimbledon four times, Australian singles championships three times, two singles Italian Crowns, The US Open, and French Open singles, twice. Between 1954 and 1973, he played and won ten of the twelve Davis Cup finals matches. He was the first player to win $1 million in prize money. Rod's other singles titles include, West Germany in 1961 and 1962, South Africa in 1969, The Canadian Open in 1970 and The U.S. Professional Indoor and World Indoor doubles championship in 1976. Laver rightfully earned his nickname because of a machine-like left arm that could hit tennis balls harder, faster and more accurately than any player of his time. His aggressive, attacking style of play still continues to influence many of today's players. It is said that Rod never hit a straight shot, his ball was constantly moving and spinning with tremendous rotation.

Laver was inducted into the Tennis Hall of Fame in Newport, Rhode Island in 1981. In 1993, the Australian Tennis Hall of Fame honored Laver by introducing a bronze bust of him to be displayed at the National Center in Melbourne, Australia.

He is an idol in the tennis world, but he had an idol too. "I guess I idolized Lew Hoad probably more than anyone because he had such power and the top-spin I felt like I wanted, but couldn't get it."

I still see Rod today at tennis matches that we both attend and enjoy, and he is as friendly and gracious, as always. He is a champion of his sport; highly respected and revered among all in the tennis communities in America and worldwide.

Rod's word of wisdom on the game, "You just hope that the tradition of the game to the young players that come along stays. I certainly respect the game and love the game. Competition is very healthy."

His competitive passion and his love for the game of tennis is what the world loves about him. So much so, that a major tennis complex was named for him in Melbourne, Australia. Rod Laver Arena is the main venue for the Australian Open, the first major tennis event every year.

Carol Lawrence
Singer – Actress
Interviewed: 2000

MY WIFE MARY JANE AND I MET the beautiful and multi-talented Carol Lawrence when Rita and Jerry Vale introduced us in the late 1990s. When we saw her again in Palm Springs in 2000 and I asked her if she would be a guest on my radio show. She agreed and was looking forward to it. After we finished the interview, we enjoyed a lovely lunch, sharing wonderful stories about people we knew and worked with in show business and fond remembrances of our Italian heritage. Carol is a first-generation Italian, both her mom and dad were born in Italy and migrated to America, like so many did for freedom and opportunity.

She is one of the few performers who defines the term 'Triple Crown.' She moved from screen roles, to live concert performances, to live theater, with the greatest of ease and talent. Carol created the role of Maria in the Leonard Bernstein classic, *West Side Story* on Broadway. "I did thirteen auditions for *West Side Story*. It's a record. So, they drafted a rule called the 'Carol Lawrence Rule' and it said that you could only audition people three times for any show, Equity show, after that, you must pay them to come in and audition." She continued, "*West Side Story* was a blessing in my life. I learned so much. Surround yourself with the very best, that was the lesson I learned from *West Side Story*. We had geniuses."

Also, on Broadway, Carol starred in, *Saratoga*, *Subways Are for Sleeping*, *Nightlife*, *I Do, I Do* and played the title role in *The Kiss of the Spider Woman*. Carol added, "The process of choosing is the most important, it's how you cast a show."

Carol played to standing room only in the national tours of *Funny Girl*, *The Unsinkable Molly Brown*, *The Sound of Music*, *Sweet Charity*, *I Do, I Do*, *No, No Nanette*, *Woman of The Year* and *Sugar Babies* with Mickey Rooney. "When the audiences left the theater, they were better off than when they came in. They were taught a lifelong lesson that will make society and their lives better." It's easy to see why the girl from Melrose Park, Illinois received her star on the Hollywood Walk of Fame, the first recipient in the category of Live Theater.

On television, Carol played leading roles on *The Commish* and *Murder She Wrote* with Angela Lansbury. She appeared on *Matt Houston, Hotel, Love Boat, Simon* and *Simon*, played the loving Italian matriarch Angela Eckhart on ABC-TVs *General Hospital, Lois and Clark, Murder One, Touched by an Angel,* and an episode of *Flipper* that was shot in Australia. The show's producers decided to make her character a recurring one, and wrote two more scripts that included her for the new season. Her other television appearances were countless musical specials and talk shows. Carol told us, "We were in the Golden Age of television at the time, 1957, '58 and '59. Every Broadway show emanated from New York City, with so many platforms that you could sing and dance."

Lawrence hosted her own bi-weekly television magazine/talk show, *The Carol Lawrence Show,* for four years, which she wrote and produced for the Trinity Broadcasting Network. The show's theme song, "In His Spotlight," set the stage for showcasing celebrities, cooking, nutrition, fashion, exercise, children, music and other interesting topics.

Carol's nightclub act dazzled crowds from Las Vegas to Toronto. Her eight-week booking of *Sugar Babies* in Harrah's Casino in Atlantic City, New Jersey, ran for five months. She also performed with the most prestigious symphony orchestras in America and Canada.

Lawrence performed as a regular on various cruise ships, including the Norwegian and Royal Caribbean Cruise Lines. Carol also enjoyed teaching aerobic exercise classes on board the ships to enthusiastic passengers.

In her personal life, Carol faced the challenges of raising two sons as a single parent, taking them on the road with her in the 1980s. Carol shared a personal lesson about herself during our interview, "I'm a very good student and when somebody's telling me the truth and it works, but if what they said to me doesn't work, you don't have my attention anymore." She wrote her autobiography, *Carol Lawrence – The Backstage Story*, sharing her life in and out of the entertainment industry and as a role model for others who believe that they too, can do it all.

Carol is a Triple Crown winner as an actress- singer- entertainer. She's a sure bet!

Robert Loggia
Actor
Interviewed: 2000

I met character actor; Robert Loggia in the late 1950s at a celebrity softball game at Roxbury Park in Beverly Hills, California. It was a pickup game that we played every Sunday, mostly with actors, producers and directors. Robert played third base. I recall he had very good hands and a strong throwing arm. We had much in common, including tennis and we played a lot of men's doubles tennis matches for years. He played competitively and was a good sport. In 2000, I asked him if he would be a guest on my radio show and he gladly accepted. We recorded the show at his home in Bel Air, California. Robert and I remained good friends until he passed away in 2015, at the age of 85.

Going back to his beginnings, Robert shared, "As a sophomore, I went to college on a football scholarship. When I was 18 years old, a professor asked me to do Petruchio in *Taming of the Shrew*. I did the play and instantaneously it was a 'calling.' I knew I wanted to be an actor." After college, Loggia went into the military for two years. "When I got out of the Army, I ran into a buddy who became an agent. It's like God's looking down on you and directing your life, so to speak. I studied with Stella Adler and got my first role in *Somebody Up There Likes Me*, co-starring with Paul Newman. You never know where luck is gonna come." Coincidentally, it was my first film too, in 1956. It was also Steve McQueen's film debut.

Robert's very successful career began when he played Frankie Machine in the off-Broadway play, *The Man with the Golden Arm*. That led to starring Broadway roles in *Toys in The Attic*, *Three Sisters*, and David Rabe's *Boom, Boom, Boom*.

It wasn't long before Disney Studios cast him as the dashing Western hero in the television series, *The Nine Lives of Elfego Baca*, which lasted three seasons. Robert said, "I learned how to be a gunslinger, ride horses; I had great teachers. It was like a childhood fantasy to do westerns." He later starred as Thomas Hewitt Edward Cat in the series, *The Cat,* which ran for three seasons.

Robert's career segued back and forth from television to films. He received an ACE Award nomination for Best Actor portraying William Kuntsler in HBO's, *The Trial of the Chicago Eight*. He also co-starred in the miniseries, *Favorite Son* and a television series entitled, *Mancuso FBI,* that earned him an Emmy nomination. Robert was busy doing several movies for television, *White Male* for HBO, *Joan of Arc*, a four-hour miniseries for CBS, *Jake Lassiter,* a movie of the week for NBC, and a miniseries, *Wild Palms,* produced by Oliver Stone. He guest-starred in four segments of the *Sopranos* television series as the character Feech La Manna.

Loggia became one of the most in-demand character actors in *An Officer and a Gentleman* in 1982, *Scarface* in 1983 and *Jagged Edge* in 1985, for which he received an Academy Award nomination. More outstanding work followed in *Prizzis' Honor*. Robert shared, "In *Prizzi's Honor*, we had two weeks of rehearsal. That's how you discover your character, through rehearsal. I don't know why more films don't do that; they should rehearse."

His other fine performances were in *Gaby, Over the Top, Triumph of The Spirit, The Marrying Man, Necessary Roughness, Gladiator, Innocent Blood, Bad Girls, Man with a Gun, Independence Day, Lost Highway, Holy Man, I Dreamed of Africa, Return to Me* and *All Over Again*.

As an actor, Loggia shared, "You're creating your palette as an actor, all the colors you know you can deal with to create a character." One of the most memorable scenes in Robert's career was when he danced on the piano in *Big*, with Tom Hanks. Loggia's comment about that wonderful film was simply, "It worked out to perfection."

Somebody Up There Likes Me was our first film. We both loved to play tennis and enjoyed our successes in show business and all the fun we shared. Robert and I had a lot in common, memories and a friendship, that I'll always cherish.

Robert expressed, "I've always worked as an actor. I've been extremely fortunate. I've had a very well-rounded, interesting career." He continued, "There's nothing, nothing more precious than individual freedom of expression and the freedom of your life's endeavor to choose what you want to do with your life."

Trini López III
Singer – Entertainer – Actor
Interviewed: 2000

I met singer, entertainer Trini López when he landed his first job singing at Marshall Edson's Ye Little Club in Beverly Hills, California. It was an intimate hotspot for up-and-coming entertainers to showcase their talents. I knew the owner Marshall Edson very well and when Trini finished his last song, Marshall brought him to my table and introduced us. We became friends from that night to this present day, some 60 years later. Coincidently, we both eventually moved to the beautiful Palm Springs area and over the years, saw each other at many dinner parties, social and charity events and loved to reminisce about the good 'ol days.

In the beginning of our interview, we were talking about the past and the path that Trini took to stardom. He told us about working on stage with the Beatles. "I was working with them at the Olympia, a three-week engagement in Paris. They sang 'I Wanna Hold Your Hand' and I sang 'If I Had a Hammer.' He told us that The Beatles were fans and added, "Fate is so interesting. Destiny is such a great thing in life."

López traveled a long way from his humble beginnings in the barrios of Dallas, Texas when a group called The Crickets befriended him. They sent him two hundred dollars to join them in Hollywood. They asked him to be their lead singer after Buddy Holly was killed in a tragic plane crash along with Richie Valens and The Big Bopper. Trini used the money sent by The Crickets to drive his station wagon to California. "It took me three days to get there and I was very scared, but I kept saying, Hollywood or bust!"

The agreement Trini had with The Crickets didn't materialize and the two hundred dollars he left Dallas with, was gone. He heard about the Ye Little Club and drove to Beverly Hills, auditioned for owner Marshall Edson and got the job. His engagement was supposed to be for two weeks. It lasted for a year. "Sure enough, I finished my engagement, I get a call from the owner of PJ's and he said, 'I'd like you to come and work for us.'" He was on

to the celebrated PJ's nightclub, in Hollywood. López started gaining a large following. "I was extended for three months and was booked for a year." Don Costa, a record producer for Reprise Records, heard about the excitement Trini was creating at PJ's, taped his act and played it for the principle owner of the company, Mr. Frank Sinatra. The great singer recognized his talent and immediately signed López to an exclusive eight-year contract. The rest is history.

Trini López's first big hit, "If I Had a Hammer" went to gold, followed by "I'm Coming Home Cindy," "Michael," "Lemon Tree," "Kansas City," "America" and "La Bamba." He tallied twenty-eight international hit singles and forty-eight albums. They included *Trini Lopez Live at PJ's*, *Trini Lopez Live in London*, *Trini Lopez's Greatest Hits*, the *Best of Trini Lopez*, *Trini Lopez Dance Party* and *Trini Lopez: 25th Anniversary Album*. He expressed, "I did all kinds of venues, I did a little bit of everything. What a grind I had and did it for twenty years." But added that, "A singer has got to have not just one hit, not just two, but many in order to stay in the business."

Trini was discovered as a talented actor. He began by playing a priest and a parole officer on two of Jack Webb's, *Adam 12* shows for Universal Studios. He appeared in two cameos, *Marriage on The Rocks*, starring Frank Sinatra, Dean Martin and Deborah Kerr and *A Poppy is Also a Flower,* starring Sean Connery, Angie Dickinson and Grace Kelly. He became an Army G.I. for a TV movie of the week called, *The Reluctant Heroes* for Aaron Spelling Productions and landed his first co-starring role in *Antonio* with actor Larry Hagman.

Trini followed with a role in the classic 1967 film, *The Dirty Dozen* starring Telly Savalas, Lee Marvin and Charles Bronson. He said, "When I was doing *The Dirty Dozen,* I did an album, one of my big hits, *Trini Lopez in London*. After completion of *The Dirty Dozen,* I had many parties in my penthouse in Hollywood. They all came to my parties, a lot."

López spoke about the actresses in Hollywood he worked with in his cameo roles, "Grace Kelly, Princess Grace of Monaco and Deborah Kerr were gorgeous and so down to earth. Beautiful to be with them, they were humble. I wish more ladies would take note of that."

A very special tribute was given to Trini when he was honored on the floor of Congress in Washington D.C., as a Goodwill Ambassador for the United States and for his charitable work throughout the world. Trini shared, "I did it with my music. That was the main reason with many songs that have to do with goodness, love and patriotism. I love America."

Every time my wife Mary Jane and I saw my long-time friend, Trini, we shared big smiles, big hugs and always had so many nice things to recollect about the past, present and looking to the future. Trini said of his life and successful career, "All of the things I wanted to do, they all came true for me. Can you believe it?" Yes, I can. Trini López was that talented and that deserving.

Sadly, Trini passed away on Aug. 11, 2020 at the age of 83.

Maurice Lucas

National Basketball Association – Portland Trailblazer Hall of Fame

Interviewed: 1998

I MET MAURICE LUCAS for the first time when he hosted The Annual AmeriFirst Big Gig Celebrity Golf Challenge in the beautiful Palm Springs, California area, and it was a huge success. The celebrities that were invited were former players from the National Basketball Association, former Major League Baseball, former National Football League and several motion picture and television stars. Signing autographs and lots of great golf kept all of us busy throughout the weekend.

Maurice Lucas attended Portland State University where he became an All-American basketball player in 1972, 1973, and 1974. Looking back, Maurice said, "I was the second fastest swimmer when I was twelve years old in the state of Pennsylvania. So, I got accustomed to being in front of a crowd on a real intense level at a very young age." His professional basketball career began with the Kentucky Colonels and later with the St. Louis Spirits in the American Basketball Association before he joined the NBA's Portland Trail Blazers in 1976. The following season, 1977, the Portland Trail Blazers won the NBA Championship. Maurice went on to make the NBA All-Star Team five times and All-Pro four times. Lucas' tenacious defensive and offensive playing earned him the label, The Enforcer. He was without question the prototype power forward of the 1970s.

With all of his successes, Maurice spoke about his heroes. "One of my heroes was Dave DeBusschere, who could shoot the outside shot and Paul Silas, who can go inside and rebound with the best of them. Then there was a guy named Chet Walker, who had a baseline jump shot. If I could combine their games, I could be successful."

NBA Hall of Famer Dave DeBusschere died in 2003 at the age of 63 from a heart attack. But Lucas saved his greatest praise for Hall of Fame guard, Oscar Robertson. He said, "When

you look at the real picture, Oscar Robertson was probably the finest player that ever played this game. No one was as steady as Oscar Robertson."

In 1973, Maurice represented the USA in The World University Games in Moscow, Russia. He received many athletic awards during and after his career, The Nike Walk of Fame, Portland Trailblazers Hall of Fame, The NBA National Spirit of Love Award for community involvement, and The Abram Distinguished Citizen Emmanuel Hospital Foundation Award in 1995. "I think the key to anyone who's wanting to achieve anything in life, it's the discipline. Discipline to me is a commitment."

After his playing days were over, Maurice became assistant coach for the Trailblazers, handling various duties such as scouting, reporting statistical information, utilizing a word processor and computers. He appeared in many television commercials, was the NBA Players Association Vice President for seven years, Ex-NBA players Association Board of Directors, served on the Advisory Board of Portland State University, an Urban League Board Member, National Minority Business Association Member, United Way National Spokesman and hosted The Annual AmeriFirst Big Gig Celebrity Golf Challenge.

The records show that Maurice Lucas was an all-star, all-pro in professional basketball. He also possessed great leadership qualities on the teams he played with, in his community and throughout the country.

Our interview was a testament to how outstanding Maurice Lucas was, on and off the court. But Lucas conceded, "No matter how great you are, and if you're playing in a team concept, you need a team around you in order to win."

The Enforcer left us way too soon. He died in 2010 at the age of 58 from bladder cancer. But he left behind a worthy legacy, that will live on for a very long time.

Carol Lynley
Actress
Interviewed: 2005

THE FIRST TIME I MET THE LOVELY ACTRESS Carol Lynley, was in 1965 at the cast reading table of Bill Sargent's Electronivision movie production of *Harlow* at Goldwyn Studios in Hollywood, California. The cast was assembled and introductions were in order. It was an excellent ensemble of stars including, Efrem Zimbalist Jr, Ginger Rogers, Barry Sullivan, Heard Hatfield, Lloyd Bochner, Hermione Baddeley, Audrey Totter, John Williams, Audrey Christie, Jack Kruschen, Celia Lovsky, Robert Strauss, Sonny Liston, and me, who played the gigolo lover of Jean Harlow in the film. Electronivision was filmed live like a stage play with multiple cameras. The film was directed by the very talented Alex Segal and produced by Lee Savin and Bill Sargent.

Lynley was perfectly cast for the role and with the beautiful platinum blonde wig and her makeup, she looked exactly like Jean Harlow; it was uncanny. Carol did an excellent job portraying the complex character, dominated by a very possessive stage mother. Unfortunately, the film was not a financial success. Most likely this was due to the Paramount Studios production of *Harlow* starring Carroll Baker. I really enjoyed working on our version because it was like performing a stage play, yet very different and exciting. Carol said, "In *Harlow*, regarding Electronivision, it was experimental. The idea of it was to rehearse it like a play and then shoot it in two days." Carol began her career as a child model at the age of 10. Two years later she made the transition from child model to cover girl. She was photographed by the best photographers for many magazines, including Richard Avedon and Horst P. Horst, and she made the cover of the top magazine at the time, *LIFE* magazine. At 15, she retired from modeling to concentrate solely on her acting career.

She was born Carol Anne Jones in New York City. It was suggested she change her last name to Lynley. Her acting career started on the Broadway stage at the age of 12 in *Blue Denim* and later starred in the film version of the play. Her other Broadway appearances

were *Anniversary Waltz* and *The Potting Shed* for which she won a Theater World Award. She also starred in *Of Mice and Men* at the Kennedy Center in New York City and starred in an off Broadway run of *The Seagull*.

Carol left the theater to star in her first motion picture, *The Light in Forest*, for Walt Disney Studios. Carol shared with me and our listening audience that, "In my first picture, *Light in the Forest*, I had a mad crush on James Mc Arthur. He's a sweetheart and it was really nice working with Jimmy."

Carol went on to appear in over fifty five motion pictures and approximately two hundred television shows. Some of her films include, *Blue Denim, Return to Peyton Place, Under the Yum Yum Tree, Bunny Lake Is Missing, The Poseidon Adventure, Washington Affair, The Cat and The Canary, Dark Tower, Vigilante,* and the film we did together, *Harlow.* Carol remarked, "I've done fifty-five films and *Bunny Lake is Missing* is my personal favorite."

Some of Lynley's episodic television appearances include, *Alfred Hitchcock Presents, Run for Your Life, Man from Uncle, Big Valley, Mannix, Police Woman, Kojak, Fantasy Island, Hawaii Five-0, Love Boat, The Fall Guy, Hart to Hart, The FBI, The Invaders, Man From Uncle, The Virginian* and the list goes on and on. She also appeared on many talk and variety shows throughout her career.

Carol talked about filming *The Poseidon Adventure*, the 1972 blockbuster that started the disaster movie trend. "The first two weeks of being dry and then three-and-a-half months of being wet! The sets in the beginning were right side up and then they were upside down."

Working with so many actors and actresses, Carol said that, "I kind of bond with almost everyone I work with because as you know, it's an intimate hands-on collaboration when you're working." She added, "It's not only the story of the movie, it's the time you spend with them, the cast and everyone, it was a learning experience. She shared her thoughts about working with two famous actors, Lawrence Olivier and Noel Coward. "Lawrence Olivier was very 'jokey.' He told jokes, showed pictures of his kids and did a soft-shoe dance. Noel Coward was a very kind-hearted, lovely guy."

The pixie, talented Carol Lynley will be missed by all her fans, friends and those of us who had the special pleasure of knowing and working with her. She was a delight and I will always remember her professionalism and how easy it was for us to work together.

Carol believed, "Growth comes from living your life." And she did so, beautifully, until she passed away in 2019 at the age of 77.

35

James MacArthur
Actor
Interviewed: 1995

I CANNOT BELIEVE IT'S BEEN OVER 35 YEARS since I first met actor James MacArthur, who would eventually become one of my best friends. We met at a celebrity charity tennis tournament in the San Fernando Valley, in California. I would see Jim (he preferred to be called Jim, not James) from time to time at various tennis and golf charity events in Los Angeles. Many years later, coincidentally, we both moved to the Palm Springs, California, area. It didn't take long before we were both invited to the same celebrity golf tournaments in the area and around the country. In between those events, we played golf together twice a week and joined a show business lunch bunch where met once a week when we could. Jim's wife, H.B. Dunz, played golf on the women's professional tour for 10 years before she met him in Hawaii. I was very lucky and grateful to receive free professional lessons when she played golf with us! H.B. and their son, Jamie, were terrific golfers and challenging opponents. We all socialized and saw each other on many occasions through the years until Jim left us far too soon.

James MacArthur began his career in the professional theater at the age of 10, appearing in *The Corn is Green*. At the age of 18, he won the title role in the CBS television production, *Deal A Blow*. The next year the studio made the story into a movie entitled, *The Young Stranger*, starring Jim and directed by John Frankenheimer. Soon thereafter, he signed a three-picture deal with Disney Studios, beginning with *Light in The Forest, Third Man on The Mountain,* and *Swiss Family Robinson*. About *Swiss Family Robinson*, Jim said, "It was a wonderful, incredible experience on Tobago Island. We were there for six months going to work every day, swinging on ropes. Work doesn't get any better than that!"

In between films, Jim made his Broadway debut in Arthur Laurent's *Invitation to a March*, playing opposite Jane Fonda.

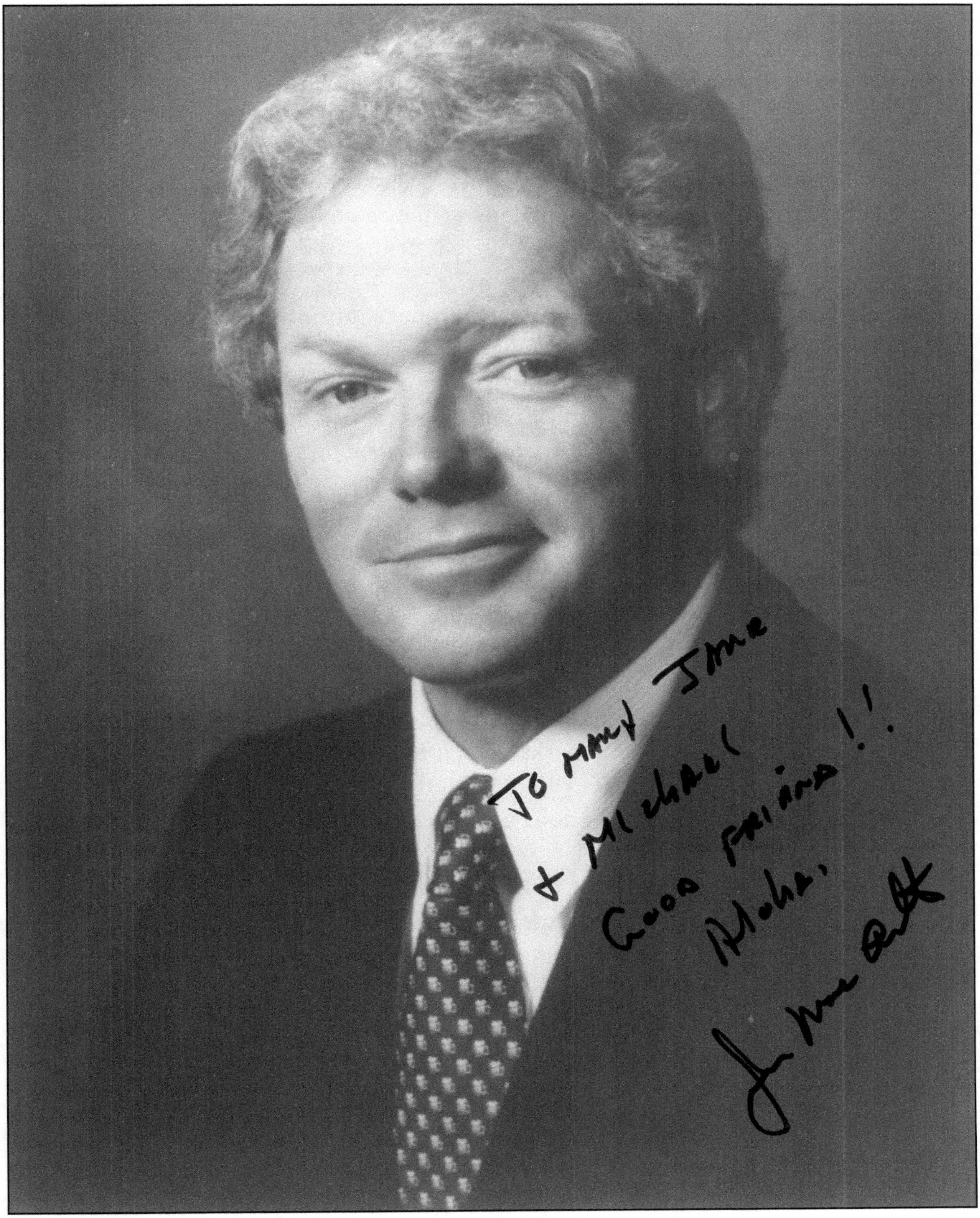
To Mary Jane
& Michael
Good friends!!
Aloha,

After which, he starred in such movies as *The Interns*, *Spencer's Mountain* with Henry Fonda and Maureen O'Hara, followed by *The Truth About Spring* opposite Hayley Mills, *Cry of Battle* with Van Heflin, *The Bedford Incident* with Sidney Poitier and Richard Widmark and *The Battle of the Bulge* with Henry Fonda. He guest starred in many hit television series. They included *The Untouchables, Gunsmoke, Wagon Train, The 11th Hour, The Great Adventure, Love Boat, Fantasy Island, Vegas,* and *Walking Tall*.

Regarding his experience with character actors and actresses, Jim's take was, "I think in the old days, my analogy, like a symphony orchestra and different notes and different instruments would play and they'd have different colors. Today, everybody's playing the drums. Everybody blaring out at the same time."

In 1968, Leonard Freeman, the creator and producer of *Hawaii Five-0*, offered him the part of the detective, Dan Williams, better known as 'Dano.' That show was one of the most successful in the history of television and Hawaii was his home for the next eleven years. *Hawaii Five-0* played in over 100 countries and aired for twelve seasons. It was number one in the television ratings, not only in the USA but in England, France, Germany, Japan, and many other countries.

Jim returned to the theater in the national tour of Jean Kerr's *Lunch Hour* with Cybill Shepherd. This was followed by the national tour of *Arsenic and Old Lace* playing Mortimer to Jean Stapleton's and Marion Ross's doting aunties.

MacArthur's special interest was traveling. He ventured to the far corners of the earth, including Russia, China, South America, and Europe, where he climbed the Matterhorn, and in Australia, he scaled Ayres Rock.

Jim drove from London to South Africa in a Land Rover, camped across the Sahara Desert, the rain forests and game parks, which took five months and covered 18,000 miles. Jim told us about the Sahara, "Endless to the horizon, just flat as a pancake." He added, "I traveled a great deal and I don't go first class. I like to get into the back country and rough it."

His mother is the late 'First Lady of the Theater,' actress Helen Hayes. His father, the late playwright Charles MacArthur, wrote award-winning classic films such as, *Wuthering Heights, Front Page* and *Gunga Din*.

About his father, Jim shared, "My father, our times spent together were at midnight when he couldn't sleep and he'd come in the room and wake me up and say, 'C'mon, let's talk,' and he would sit and tell me stories of his life and the next thing I knew it's three or four in the morning, and I had to go to school when he could sleep all morning. I treasure those moments."

And about his mom, "She insisted, not when I was sixteen years old mind you, but later, to get some lessons and work on it. I never did anything in the theater with her. We did a Tarzan together down in Mexico and of course, my mother did two *Hawaii 5-0's*. It was great to work with her. We were very close. She was involved in so many things. She was a letter-writer, raised roses, did needlepoint."

James MacArthur was a man for all seasons and a true friend. I miss him and will always remember all the good times we shared. And I'll never forget the morning of Sept. 11, 2001, when the phone rang at seven o'clock in the morning and we heard Jim's voice saying, "Turn on the TV."

Jim passed away in 2010 at age 72, but I can tell you this: he made the most of every moment.

Gavin & Patti MacLeod
Actor – Actress
Interviewed: 1996

I MET GAVIN MACLEOD AND HIS TALENTED WIFE, PATTI, quite some time ago in Rancho Mirage, California. The first time I saw Gavin, he was starring in a dramatic play with Robert Blake called *The Connection* in a small theater in Hollywood, California in 1957. He was excellent in the role of 'Mother' and received great reviews. When I walked out of the theater that evening, I promised myself that whenever I did meet Gavin, I would tell him how much I enjoyed his work and that he had a great future as an actor. It was many years later that we finally met and he was so appreciative and got such a kick out of my waiting to tell him about it, because he too thought it was one of his best performances. Gavin went on to appear in many other stage shows. They include *Carousel, A Funny Thing Happened on The Way to The Forum, Gypsy, Annie Get Your Gun*, and a national tour of the hit show, *Love Letters,* to sold-out performances. A sixteen-week run in Montréal, Canada of *The Sisters Rosenzweig* and a highly successful summer tour of *Showboat* is where he garnered rave reviews.

Television beckoned Gavin in 1970 to the *Mary Tyler Moore Show* playing Murray Slaughter and is considered a classic. It wasn't long after that show ended his comedic talents catapulted him to star in the long-running successful series, *The Love Boat* (1977-1987), playing Captain Stubing.

It became a huge fan favorite, literally around the world. He still remains the most famous ship captain to millions, everywhere. Gavin said, "You know what it did? It created an industry. Everybody cruises today or talks about cruising today. It wasn't that way before the *Love Boat* was on the air."

Gavin has appeared in many classic films such as *I Want to Live, The Sand Pebbles, Compulsion and Kelly's Heroes*. Over the years he's been a triple nominee for 'Best Actor in a Comedy Series' by the Hollywood Foreign Press.

He has continued his long and treasured association with Princess Cruise Lines, making guest appearances. He considers this association an extension of himself in many ways as he loves to travel with his wife and they consider every cruise an adventure in their pursuit of maintaining a healthy, relevant and romantic marriage. Gavin spoke from his heart, "And you know, because of the pressures of today, I don't know how people do it, you know, they do it without having the same spiritual life."

Patti MacLeod's career began in her hometown of Washington, D.C., where she danced with the Washington School of Ballet. On the West Coast, she danced with the Santa Monica Civic Ballet in *The Merry Widow, The Chocolate Soldier, Fanny, Three Penny Opera and Guys and Dolls*. Patti exclaimed, "Actors need a reason, a motivation. Dancers just say 'OK' and just do it!"

Patti's numerous television credits include the Emmy award-winning *That Certain Summer*. Patti and Gavin have worked on stage together in *The Seven Year Itch, Never Too Late, Chapter Two, The Last of The Red-Hot Lovers, and Annie Warbucks*. Gavin shared about being on the stage, "For me, doing a play, being on that stage in front of people, and so for that first time early, that's where the career is. Patti and I do shows all over, wherever."

Patti and Gavin spoke about their perceptions of television for children and adult viewers. Patti said, "Television that gives something to work up to. Is it better to give them a happy-ever-after program or that something is so violent? There's gotta be something in the middle." Gavin added, "There's gotta be a sense of moral responsibility and I think the more we don't have that, the country goes down the tubes. Now they have to see everything so there's no imagination left to the kids." Patti has hope, saying, "CBS is the network changing. They give them a chance, especially *Touched by an Angel* has a chance. They are seeing that, like *Dr. Quinn*, in other series."

The MacLeod's appeared weekly on the Trinity Broadcasting Network in their series *Back on Course,* a five-time Religion in Media-Award Winner and the recipients of the International Communications Galaxy of Fame Award. They have been truly blessed to be together and live a long-lasting and creative life.

I am blessed to call Patti and Gavin MacLeod my friends. It was an honor to have interviewed them together, on my radio show. That was some years ago and we are still friends to this day. And I know, from a religious point of view, the captain of their ship, is the Lord.

The captain called Gavin home on May 29, 2021.

Virginia Mayo
Actress
Interviewed: 1995

I MET THE BEAUTIFUL ACTRESS VIRGINIA MAYO in the makeup department at Warner Bros. Studios in Burbank, California in the late 1950s. We were both there to test for our makeup color and balance in preparation for the filming of *Westbound*. It was my first starring role in a motion picture, thanks to director Budd Boetticher, who cast me in the role of Rod. Virginia looked as pretty without makeup as she did with it. She was very charming to wish me good luck and said she was looking forward to working together on the film. I was a big fan of hers and those nice words were very encouraging, coming from a star of her stature. The first day of shooting she made me feel important and part of the family of actors who were cast in the film. That goes a long way with a newcomer and I'll forever remember her kindness.

Virginia Mayo decided she wanted a career in show business at the age of six. Her first role as an actress, singer and dancer began with the St. Louis Municipal Opera Company. Virginia said, "I was a chorus girl. I did a whole season of musicals and I was only 17 years old. One musical after another. It was great training and I was in seventh heaven." Shortly thereafter, she toured the country in a musical comedy act called, *Pansy the Horse*. Tired of being on the road, she joined Billy Roses' new review at his famous Diamond Horseshoe Nightclub. Legendary producer Samuel Goldwyn immediately signed her to an exclusive contract after seeing her perform *Princess and The Pirate* at the nitery. Virginia shared with our listening audience, "The first musical I did was with James Cagney in *The West Point Story*. I was dancing in the movie."

During her tenure with Goldwyn Studios, she appeared in several motion pictures including *The Best Years of Our Lives*, *She's Working Her Way Through College*, *Capt. Horatio Hornblower* with Gregory Peck and a series of musical comedies opposite Danny Kaye.

These included *The Secret Life of Walter Mitty, The Kid from Brooklyn, Wonder Man* and *A Song Is Born*.

About MGM, Virginia added, "At first, Gene Nelson did a couple of dance numbers with me. I just loved dancing. It was my whole life, really. Gene and I starred in six movies together."

After her contract ran out at Goldwyn Studios, Virginia signed a lucrative contract with Warner Bros. Studios, where she became their top moneymaking star for several years.

Among her personal favorites made for Warner Bros. were *She's Back on Broadway* with Gene Nelson, *Colorado Territory* with Joel McCrea, *White Heat* opposite James Cagney and *The Iron Mistress* with Alan Ladd. She has starred opposite some of Hollywood's finest leading men such as Rex Harrison, Paul Newman, Burt Lancaster, Kirk Douglas, Ronald Reagan, Randolph Scott, Robert Stack and Gregory Peck.

Virginia recalled, "Of all the dramatic actors I worked with, I thought Gregory Peck was one of the finest." About comedy she said, "Comedy is more difficult. Drama is easy. You just do it the way you would feel it normally. In comedy, you have to have special techniques. I learned an awful lot when I was in vaudeville about comedy. The timing is so important in comedy. In comedy, Bob Hope was the ultimate. He was the most fun."

Mayo delighted theater audiences throughout the country with her lovely voice and dancing talents in *Forty Carats, Hello Dolly, Butterflies Are Free, No, No Nanette, Fiorello, Cactus Flower and Tunnel of Love*. She also guest-starred on many television shows throughout her lengthy and successful career, as well.

In her spare time, Virginia liked to paint in oils and watercolors. Above all, she enjoyed the company of her family and her beautiful home in the San Fernando valley area of Southern California. She passed away at the age of 84 in 2005.

Virginia Mayo was supremely talented, charming, friendly and highly professional to work with. I learned so much about her life and career in show business during our interview with one special thing she shared that will always stay with me. Virginia told me, off mike, that her favorite sandwich was peanut butter and jelly. How very sweet of her to share that personal delight. For all of her beauty, class and refinement, Virginia was still just down to earth, underneath it all.

Barbara McNair
Entertainer – Actress
Interviewed: 1995

I MET ENTERTAINER, ACTRESS BARBARA MCNAIR at the Dennis James Celebrity-Charity Golf Classic in Palm Springs, California. It didn't take long to get to know Barbara; she was charming, with an effervescent personality. She was one of only a few female celebrities that participated in many charity tournaments by playing golf and performed as an entertainer.

I hosted my own charity golf tournament for eight years in the 1990s in the Palm Springs area, The Michael Dante Celebrity Golf Classic, where Barbara played golf and also performed at the dinner gala, always to an adoring audience. Her participation helped to raise funds to benefit the different charities my tournament supported. When I asked Barbara to be a guest on my radio show, she readily accepted. We were friends for many years until she passed away in 2007 at age 72, leaving us much too soon.

Barbara McNair was one of the finest nightclub entertainers and singers in show business. She was voted one of the world's ten most beautiful women by the International Society of Cosmetologists, the first black woman to be chosen. Barbara's musical talents were evident at a very early age. Her parents enrolled her at the Racine Conservatory of Music in Wisconsin and later went to the American Conservatory of Music in Chicago. After graduation, she attended the University of California Los Angeles for one year and then decided to pursue her career in New York City.

Barbara spoke about growing up and wanting to perform. "It was the influence of television; it was in my life when I was a child. I saw people on television and wanted to be on television. I started singing when I was three years old. Once I got into college, I realized it had nothing to do with what I was interested in. I wanna just sing."

McNair worked as a secretary before her singing break came. She said, "Every spare moment I had after work, lunch hour, wherever, I would go and audition somewhere. At

To Mary Jane & Michael
It's been a pleasure being on the show!
Love
Barbara McNair
11/25/95

one lunch hour, I auditioned for Max Gordon. Max called and said, I see a spark in you. I wanna give you a chance." McNair's first opportunity came when Max Gordon of the Village Vanguard offered her a job, which led to a week's stint on *The Arthur Godfrey Show*. That was the perfect showcase for her and led to Barbara headlining at one of the top nightclubs in New York, The Purple Onion, which proved to be the turning point in her career. She went on to headline in the most prestigious nightclubs, from New York to California. We're talking The Persian Room at New York's Plaza Hotel, The Coconut Grove in Los Angeles and many of the major hotels in Las Vegas. Walter Winchell began writing about Barbara after seeing her perform at the Silver Slipper in Las Vegas, Nevada. Barbara said it got her a lot of work. "It was exciting to have that recognition at that time."

Barbara made her Broadway debut in the Harnick-Bock musical, *The Body Beautiful*. She shared with us, "I broke the color barrier on Broadway." The musical won her overwhelming critical acclaim. From there, she became the host of her own television show, *The Schaefer Circle,* had a hit record, "Bobby" with Coral Records and recorded with Signature and Motown Records.

McNair performed in two stage productions with Nat King Cole, *I'm with You* at the Greek Theater in Los Angeles and *The Merry World of Nat King Cole*. She remarked, "Nat had perfect pitch. A gift from God, something you are born with. He was such a wonderful musician." Incidentally, his daughter, Natalie Cole made her stage debut, playing Miss McNair as a young girl.

Barbara went on to Richard Roger's Broadway hit, *No Strings* in New York with Richard Kiley and then on the national tour with Howard Keel.

She appeared on Broadway again in *Pajama Game* opposite Hal Linden and later performed in Berlin, Germany in *Sophisticated Lady*, a celebration of the music of Duke Ellington.

McNair's dramatic television roles included, *The Eleventh Hour, Mission Impossible, Vegas, The Jeffersons, Helltown, The Red Foxx Show,* and *Snoops*. "Acting is very much like singing, you're telling a story. You have a feeling. The more I did it, the more I loved it." Her silver screen appearances, *If He Hollers* with Raymond St. Jacques, *Stiletto* with Alex Cord, *Venus in Furs* with James Darren, *Change of Habit* with Elvis Presley and two movies with Sidney Poitier, *They Call Me Mr. Tibbs* and *The Organization*. "Sidney was so generous with his talent. He helped all of us to be better actors." She had a recurring role on the soap opera, *General Hospital* and her own television show again in 1969 and 1970, *The Barbara McNair Show*. "We were syndicated and we had to do three one-hour shows a week."

Every time Mary Jane and I heard Barbara perform, singing in her soulful and melodic style, we knew we were in the presence of a gifted, talented entertainer. Barbara was one of the nicest ladies you'd ever want to know with an irresistible smile that could light up a room.

Barbara spoke about her life and career as a performer. "I never had much of a recording career. I was more interested performing live, that gave me more pleasure. I think my life has been a wonderful thing. I really enjoyed being in this business, I'm so glad I chose this business."

We are happy she shared her talent in show business with us.

Gerald McRaney
Actor
Interviewed: 2006

THE FIRST TIME I MET AWARD-WINNING ACTOR, director, writer, producer Gerald McRaney was in 1986. It was on the set of the very successful television series he starred in, playing the likable private investigator, Rick Simon in *Simon and Simon*. I appeared as one of the guests on the show, playing a professional tennis player who might have been involved in a murder case. I had fun playing that character because for half the day I was hitting tennis balls with another player. At the time I played a lot of tennis in the Beverly Hills, California area with many of my celebrity friends. The producer of the show was a friend of mine, John Stevens, and he knew I played tennis. He called me at home and asked me if I wanted to portray a tennis player in a segment of the show. I didn't have to go through casting for the role, as John filled me in on what the story and the character was about. A few days later we were filming the episode, *Tonsillitis*.

It was years later when I called and asked Gerald if he would do an interview with me on my radio show. He gladly accepted and we went to his beautiful home in the Hollywood Hills to conduct the interview. He couldn't have been more gracious. Mary Jane and I had the pleasure of meeting his lovely, talented wife Delta Burke, as well.

Gerald McRaney has had a long and illustrious career starring in an amazing list of highly-rated television series and movies on all broadcasts and cable networks. He commented during the interview, "I've known from the age of fourteen that I wanted to be an actor. I think movies and TV are what I wanted to do from the time I was a kid."

Some of his credits include CBS-TV's *Jag*, HBO's *Deadwood*, the CBS mini-series, *Nothing Lasts Forever* and *A Stranger Beside Me*, a movie for CBS, *Deadly Vows*, NBC's *Someone She Knows* and *Dream of Murder*, the CBS suspense drama, *Fast Forward* and NBC's *Lassiter*.

He also starred with Jill Clayburn in the 2003 critically acclaimed off Broadway play, *The Exonerated*, and the list goes on.

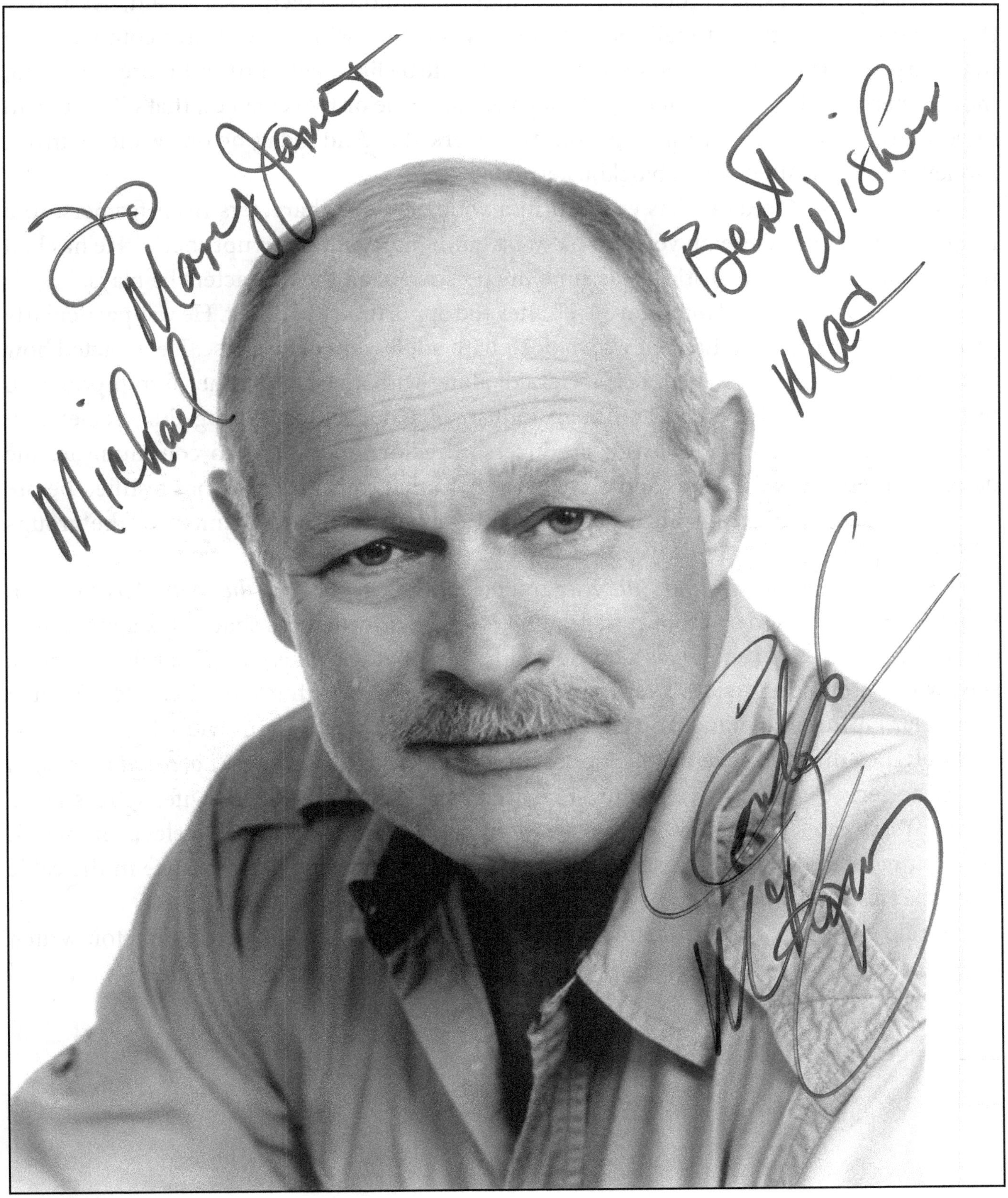
To Mary Janet Michael
Best Wishes Mac

McRaney managed to avoid the pitfalls of typecasting by paying his dues as a working actor in a myriad of stage productions, TV shows and motion pictures. He said, "As actors, there's no place for them to fail the way there was for us, with little theater companies all over the countryside. You could build your craft little by little, get a little bit more confident, more experienced, it could build up. Today you have one or two chances, that's it. You're in or you're out. You don't have an opportunity to work at it. And today, no one wants to invest money in a movie unless it's a blockbuster."

To his credit, McRaney has excelled in a wide array of characters from farmers, to a hitman, a vigilante, Vietnam veteran, old west gunfighter, and a corrupt sheriff. He has had the uncanny ability to realistically assume the persona of all the characters he plays.

The series *Simon and Simon* gave McRaney the opportunity to direct. He was particularly proud of the segment he directed which dealt with adolescent drug abuse. He depicted how drug abuse can be used to glamorize. Gerald, along with a group of other film production professionals, formed the entertainment industry's, Counsel for a Drug-Free Society, an organization dedicated to lobbying producers, directors and actors to communicate the dangers of drug abuse in films and on television. In that role, McRaney has testified before the Senate subcommittee, with investigations to obtain their endorsement of the group's efforts.

He co-wrote a *Simon and Simon* segment entitled, *I Thought the War Was Over*, in which Rick Simon suffers from post-traumatic stress disorder. He shared his approach to characterization. "My father was a house builder and that's how I approach a role. You gotta start with a solid foundation. Every time I play a role, I'm learning something new about a particular type of individual. You have, at least, helped to create an individual."

McRaney directed several episodes of *Major Dad* and a TV movie, *Love and Curses*, in which he served as executive producer, as well as co-starring with his wife, actress Delta Burke. Years later, McRaney guest-starred in the Paramount Studios television series, *Yellowstone,* starring Kevin Costner, and in another outstanding performance in the cable Netflix series, *The Shooter.*

Gerald McRaney's star still shines bright for this multi-talented actor, director, writer, producer and I'm sure we'll see more of his fine work for many years to come.

Robert Morse
Actor
Interviewed: 1995

I FIRST MET ACTOR ROBERT MORSE when he moved from New York to live and work in Hollywood in the 1970s. In between working, we played in many celebrity charity golf tournaments in the Los Angeles and Palm Springs areas.

Robert was a lot of fun to be around. He had a great sense of humor and loved sports, liked watching baseball and was a big hockey fan. Robert was born and raised in Massachusetts, so naturally he was a big Boston Bruins and Red Sox fan.

This talented man made his stellar debut on Broadway in the very successful play, *The Matchmaker*. He later repeated his role in the movie version made by Paramount Pictures. Two Tony award nominations followed for his performances in *Say Darling* and *Take Me Along*, but it was his unforgettable performance in *How to Succeed in Business Without Really Trying* in 1962 that earned him his first Tony Award. His second Tony came years later for his brilliant characterization of Truman Capote in the one-man, award-winning play, *Tru*.

I had the pleasure of seeing the play with my mother at the Booth Theater in New York City. Robert received three curtain calls to standing ovations with shouts of, "Bravo! Bravo!" He also won The Drama Desk Award and The New York Critics Award for Best Actor for his outstanding performance. Robert shared about the play, "It took a long, long time to get to know the feelings and ramifications of the script and everything it suggested. The script was 120 pages and I had to learn 120 pages of dialogue in eight weeks." Continuing, Robert spoke about memorizing all the lines, "It was at the Hasty Pudding in Boston, I called you from there, Michael, that I began, as it became to be second nature to me. I really wasn't worried what the next line would be. I could explore other things within the character. More creative than I've ever been."

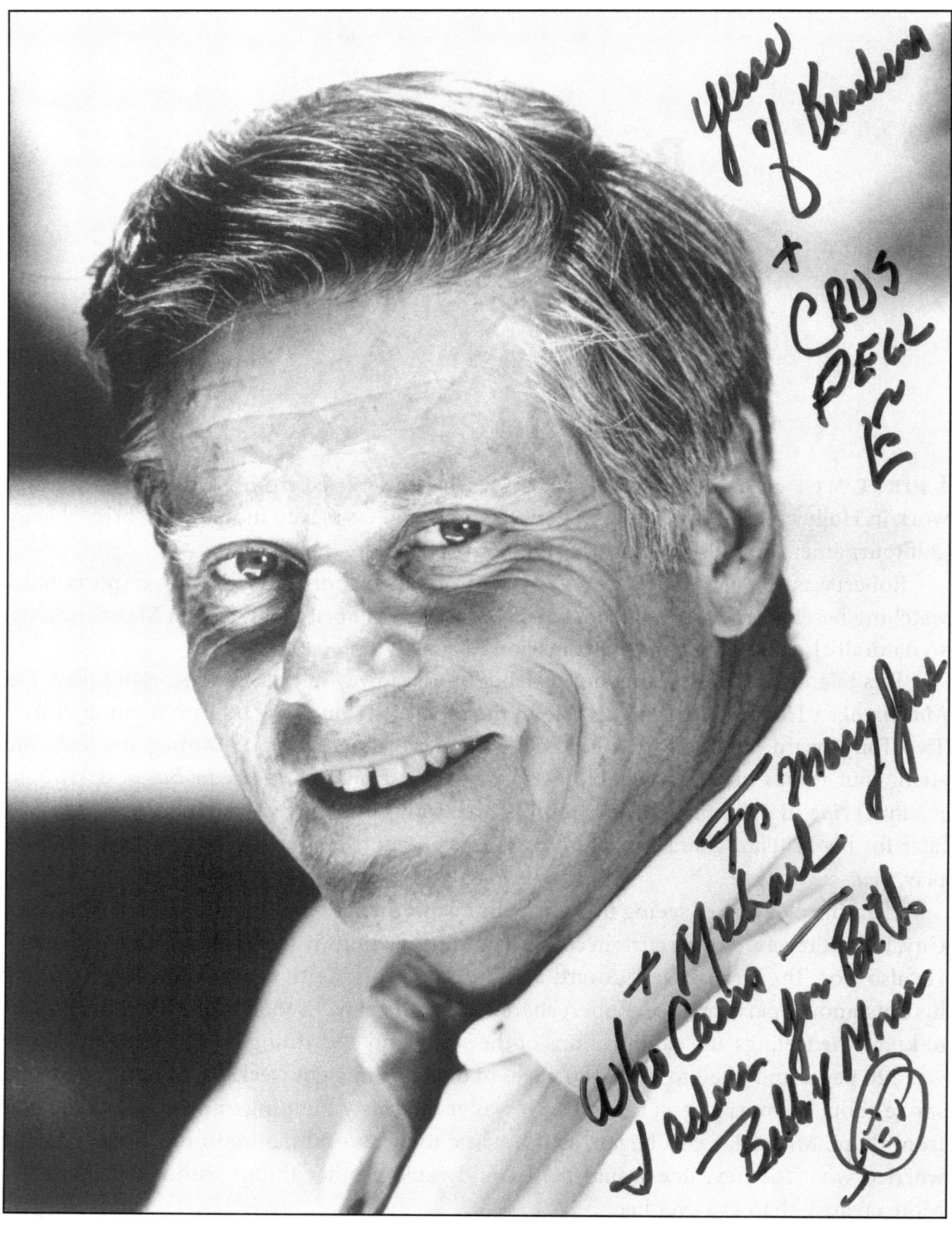

Robert starred in several motion pictures, *The Loved One, A Guide for The Married Man, Where Were You When the Lights Went Out, The Matchmaker* and of course, the film version of *How to Succeed in Business Without Really Trying.*

Television audiences remember him for his recurring role on the ABC soap opera, *All My Children*. Robert has guest-starred in TV movies, many episodic shows and miniseries. He did a great job in the mini-series, *Wild Palms*, playing the character *Chap Star Fall*, a definitive departure from any of his previous works. Morse said he also had a lot of fun playing the ghoulish Grandpa Munster in *Here Come the Munster's*, a Fox television movie based on the slightly wacky, but lovable family that graced the TV screen in the 1960s.

The stage beckoned Robert back to the comedy hit *Sugar* at The Old Vic Theater in London, starred in *Light Up the Sky* and also starred in the musical, *Showboat*, directed by Hal Prince in Toronto, Canada. Robert remembered that phone call, "Hal Prince called me collect and asked me if I would be interested in playing Captain Andy. I (quickly) said yes. It's going to go to Broadway and we're going to open in Toronto. You and Elaine Stritch are going to star, and we love you." He also commented about the cost of producing a musical, "I certainly know it's different years and years ago, but still the expense of doing a musical, you can lose six or eight million dollars in one night. In the old, old days, maybe your show can come in for one eighth, one quarter or one half of that and have a run and still make some money and get along."

Robert also performed in *Loose Lips,* a theatrical version of TVs bloopers and practical jokes played at the Santa Monica Playhouse in California. In 2007, Robert's performance in the TV series drama *Mad Men* garnered him an Emmy Award for Best Guest Actor, portraying the character, Bertram Cooper. He also received a Gold Derby TV Award and an Online Film and Television Award for Best Guest Actor in *Mad Men,* that same year.

When Robert and I were a part of the Hollywood scene, we coined the phrase, "Biggies" to describe someone that we knew or working with, that was very important in the business. Well, eventually we started calling each other "Biggies," and it's lasted to this day.

Also worthy of mention: Robert spoke lovingly about his three daughters during our interview. Two older daughters from his first wife and one from his second marriage to Libby, their daughter was only 4 1/2 years old at the time. Shortly thereafter, he and Libby had a son, Charlie, with the most beautiful red hair you've ever seen. Today, they are all adults, very proud of their dad for the outstanding award-winning work he's done on the stage, in film and on television.

"Biggies" indeed!

Don Murray

Actor

Interviewed: 2003

I MET ACTOR, WRITER, PRODUCER, DIRECTOR DON MURRAY at one of the many celebrity-charity golf events we participated in long before I was doing my radio show in Palm Springs, California. It was in 2003 when I asked Don to do my radio show and recommended recording it at his home in Santa Barbara, California. That was fine with my wife Mary Jane because we spent time in Santa Barbara over the years and always enjoyed our stay there. Don, his charming wife, Elizabeth, and his family lived on a very nice piece of property with a lot of space. Upon our arrival Don and Elizabeth made us feel right at home. After we exchanged pleasantries and set up the equipment, we recorded the show.

Don Murray began his career when he studied theater at The American Academy of Dramatic Arts, New York City, New York. He worked in small theaters, also known as 'stock' and in 1951 he debuted on Broadway in *The Rose Tattoo*. Don shared, "I was selected to play one of the four leads and that led to quite a few movies offers, which I rejected due to slave contracts. I didn't want to do that." He appeared in other plays such as *The Insect Comedy*, *The Crucible* and *Good News* before appearing on Broadway again in *The Rose Tattoo*, *The Skin of Our Teeth* with Mary Martin and Helen Hayes, *The Norman Conquests*, *Same Time, Next Year*, *The Hot Corner*, and went on major tours with *California Suite* and the musical, *Chicago*.

Murray made his motion picture debut in *Bus Stop* in 1956, co-starring opposite Marilyn Monroe. That happened because director Joshua Logan caught him in Broadway's *The Skin of Our Teeth*. "Josh Logan screen tested me for it and I got the role and that's how my career started," said Don, who received a Best Supporting actor Oscar nomination for his portrayal of a cowboy who romances Marilyn Monroe.

This was definitely his defining role as an actor and a memorable one to boot. He continued about Marilyn, "Everyone that worked with Marilyn Monroe said *Bus Stop* was

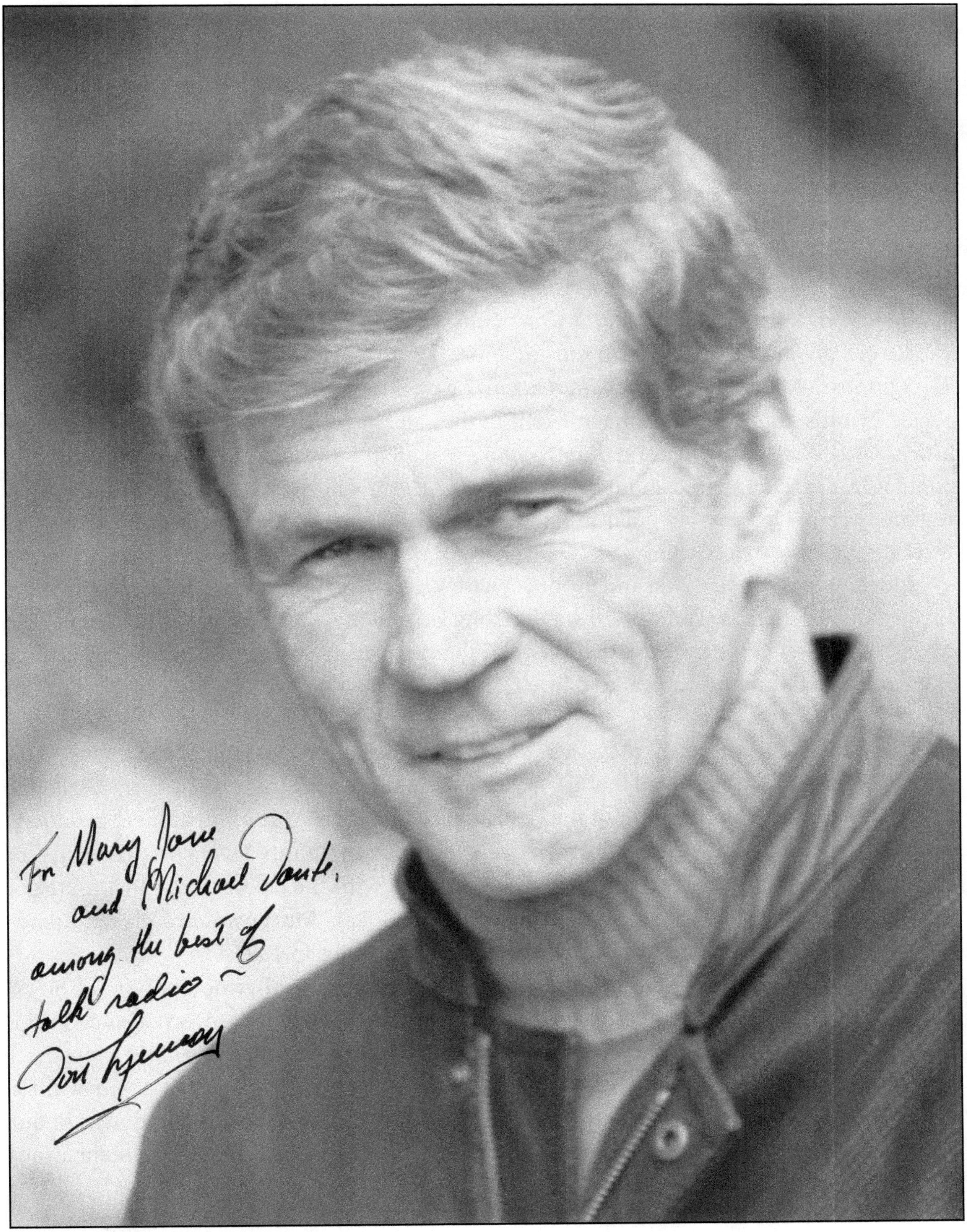

For Mary Jane
and Michael Dante,
among the best of
talk radio~
Don Murray

her 'best behaved film' since she became a star. Marilyn in *Bus Stop* was worth all the trouble because I think she was magnificent. The camera loved her."

Don went on to appear in quite a number of films beginning with *The Bachelor Party*. He noted, "In *Bachelor Party*, I played a very emotional New Yorker. I am a New Yorker!" The film roles just kept coming in the 1950s and 1960s such as *Shake Hands with The Devil, Hoodlum Priest, One's Man's Way, The Cross and The Switchblade, Conquest of the Planet of the Apes, Endless Love, Peggy Sue Got Married, Advice and Consent, Baby, The Rain Must Fall* and *Island Prey*.

Murrays' movies for television were plentiful in *Daughter of the Mind, The Intruders, Billy Budd, Winterset, The Way the West Was Won, The Stepford Children, A Girl Named Sooner, Rainbow, Crisis in Midair, Montana Crossroads, If Things Were Different, Fugitive Family, The Return of the Rebels, License to Kill* and more. His television series as a regular included, *The Outcasts*. About the series, "*The Outcasts* gave black people their first cowboy hero, played by Otis Young. He was magnificent in the role." Also, he was a regular cast member in *How the West Was Won* and *Knots Landing*, which was a spin-off of the enormously popular *Dallas*. Don shared about *Knot's Landing*, "I wrote the first two-parter for the second season." Again, Don was a regular in *Brand New Life* and *Sons and Daughters* also known as *The Hammersmith's*, for CBS.

Murray worked as a writer and producer with Joe Landon in 1960 on *The Hoodlum Priest*. He explained, "*The Hoodlum Priest* was a strong statement against capital punishment." He received The Best Actor Award at the Brussels Film Festival in 1961, The Mexico Film Festival, The San Sebastian Film Festival and The Cannes Film Festival for his fine performance in *The Hoodlum Priest*.

Don wrote and directed *The Cross and the Switchblade* with James Bonnet in 1970, starring Pat Boone. He recalled that particular movie started the movement Teen Challenge where teenagers themselves go out into communities and get kids off drugs. He produced and directed *Damien* in 1976. Murray specified about the film, "*Damien* is the story of Father Damien, a Belgian Priest who was sent to work with the lepers in the 1800s. He got leprosy himself and died in Hawaii on the island of Molokai." Murray also produced *Annie's Coming Out*, also known as *Test of Love* for Universal Studios in 1985.

Don Murray and I were both the honorees of a prestigious Hollywood honor, the Silver Spur Award, in 2006, presented by the Reel Cowboys Organization, for excellence in the western genre. This award was given to us by our peers in the entertainment industry. I always enjoyed Don's body of work and he appreciated mine, as well. It was a win-win for both of us and we were privileged to have made our way through the ups and downs of our film and television careers with success, and to have this special lifetime achievement award in common.

And like most cowboys, he deserves an award for being an all-around great guy.

Julie Newmar
Actress
Interviewed: 1996

I MET JULIE NEWMAR IN 1967, when we both guest-starred on the original *Star Trek* series. For the hardcore fans, this was Episode #32, entitled *Friday's Child*. We were cast as two other-worldly Capellans in opposition of a Klingon agent. We both wore tightfitting, very colorful green and black outfits and our body heat was extremely high in the costume fabric. As a matter of fact, I lost seven pounds during the filming and Julie, very uncomfortable playing a pregnant character, lost a few pounds, as well. The temperature that day was as high as 117 degrees where we were filming on location at Vasquez Rocks, just north of Los Angeles. We managed to survive the heat with ice packs applied to our necks and faces all day long. But at the end of the day we were happy with the results, an episode that became a fan favorite.

Julie Newmar starred in several Broadway plays, approximately twenty motion pictures, numerous episodic television shows and movies for television. Julie said about Broadway, "I always heard that if you made it on Broadway, you had a career."

She is best known for playing the character, Catwoman, in the *Batman* series, with Adam West and Burt Ward. Julie's theatrical talents are many; she learned to play the piano at a very early age, an accomplished dancer, choreographer, clothes designer, businesswoman and knows sign language. Julie, with her statuesque frame and beautiful face, once had her gorgeous legs insured for $1 million dollars, and worth every penny!

"Really, dancing was my great love. So, I started first as a pianist but then spent most development for my career in dancing. It gave me the rudimentary ability that I use best in comic timing." She added, "There's a great sense that music teaches you about timing that you need for comedy. So now, comedy is the thing I love most."

This talented lady was born and raised in Hollywood, California. Her mother was

a Ziegfeld Follies Girl and her father was a football coach and the head of the Physical Education department at Los Angeles City College. It's obvious where all her many gifts came from. Julie believed, "It doesn't matter, you know, either you get success in one way or another and then you're rewarded in a different way." For Julie, dancing was her most rewarding talent. "But all my life has been most interesting working with Jack Cole, the great choreographer."

Newmar won a Tony Award for Best Supporting Actress in the hit Broadway play, *Marriage Go-Round* with Charles Boyer. She also starred in the Broadway play *Lil Abner* and did the film adaptation for Paramount Studios playing the same character, Stupefyin' Jones. Julie starred in two films for independent producer, director William Castle, *Serpent of The Nile* and *Slaves of Babylon*, playing similar roles, dancing in both films.

Some of her other films include, *Seven Brides for Seven Brothers, The Rookie, MacKennas' Gold, Streetwalking,* and the much publicized, *To Wong Foo, Thanks for Everything! Julie Newmar.* She appeared in the high fashion runway show, Thierry Mugler Show in Paris, France, in a repeat of her first appearance there in 1992. Julie smiled, paused and said, "I was the tallest so I was always relegated to the back…hmmm!"

Newmar also took classes at UCLA, learning about real estate, finance and gardening. She also owned a fast food restaurant in the Fairfax area of Los Angeles called, Eat a Pita. The last time I saw Julie was at the Hollywood Show, an all-category autograph signing show in Los Angeles. She looked as beautiful as she always had, and her figure was still that of a dancer.

Julie shared her philosophy, "It should be your duty, it's up to you to make your part, put all your energy into that; you've gotta make it shine."

And shine, she does.

Charlie Pasarell

Association of Tennis Professionals — Tennis Hall of Fame

Interviewed: 2000

THE FIRST TIME I MET CHARLIE PASARELL JR. was at a celebrity charity tennis tournament with the San Francisco 49ers of the National Football League in Santa Cruz, California. He and another popular professional tennis player were invited to play an exhibition match to further attract tennis fans to the event.

Pasarell was a pleasure to watch with his smooth strokes, an attacking serve and volley game that led itself best to hard, indoor courts and grass courts as well. It was the first time I had the opportunity to sit courtside, to watch this extremely well-played match as they battled it out, stroke for stroke for the entire tournament. When I met Charlie, I had the opportunity to ask him some questions about the game. He could not have been nicer and more willing to share his insights. You might say, it was a free lesson from one of the top professional tennis players of his time. Charlie told me that, "Footwork is more than 50 percent of the game. You will see that all the great players, they all have great footwork." Something, as I continued to play tennis, I never forgot.

Charles M. Pasarell, Jr., known to his friends and the tennis community as 'Charlie,' was born in San Juan, Puerto Rico. Charlie played his first tennis match as a child. "I played my first game when I was eight years old, which I won. I thought I was king of the world then." Over the years, I got to know Pasarell better by playing in some of the celebrity charity tennis tournaments organized by he and his staff in the greater Palm Springs area. We also played in many of the same celebrity charity golf tournaments in the desert and on a couple of occasions we played on the same team.

Pasarell's illustrious playing career spanned over 16 years. He is the holder of eighteen singles tennis titles, including the national indoors championship twice in 1996 and 1997, as well as numerous doubles titles. He told me, "The bigger the tournament, the better I

played so I had some pretty good battles with the best and I would stand toe to toe with most of them. I'm proud of my tennis playing career."

In 1967, Charlie was ranked the number one tennis player in the United States and for five years represented the USA in the Davis Cup. The year before, Charlie founded the National Junior Tennis League along with Arthur Ashe and Sheridan Snyder. This program has exposed the sport to more than one million underprivileged children in fifty cities across the nation. He was a founding member of the Association of Tennis Professionals, a board member of the ATP Tour and inducted into the ATP Tennis Hall of Fame. Also, he was inducted into the Tennis Hall of Fame in Newport, Rhode Island and founded The Grand Champions Tennis Circuit for professional players, thirty-five years of age and over.

He was the chairman and CEO of his own company, P. M. Sports Management Corporation, along with his partner and president of his company, Raymond Moore. They designed, developed, managed and marketed sporting facilities and events. P. M. Sports, through a joint partnership with an international management group, completed a state-of-the-art tennis stadium and entertainment venue, The Indian Wells Tennis Gardens. It annually hosts The Tennis Masters Series, attracting the world's leading tennis players. "I wanna build the best possible tournament by all standards, international standards." And he did. Charlie added, "The people that work this program, they are my heroes. They do an unbelievable job. They are my heroes."

Pasarell is one of the most respected leaders and spokesmen in the world of tennis. He and his wife Shireen, married twenty years at the time of our interview, are the proud parents of their son, Charles and daughter, Fara. He is a loving husband, a dedicated father to his children, his family and his friends, on and off the court.

Case in point: March 8, 2000 was the opening day of the new tennis stadium in Indian Wells, California. Charlie designed it along with some of the most talented and experienced builders and architects. That day it was raining. Charlie had already committed to doing my radio show, but with the bad weather and opening day anticipation, I thought for sure that we would have to cancel our interview. But graciously, Charlie invited me and Mary Jane, into his office at the newly built facility. We set up the equipment, took our seats and began to talk. As we were recording, I realized what an exceptional man he was, with a sense of honor and friendship. Even though it was only about two hours before the official opening, we recorded his interview.

Charlie wanted our listeners to know the meaning of a champion to him. "A true champion is somebody that is a lion on the court, but he also keeps his cool, his temper, controls it and is a gentleman."

He is most definitely all of those things, and my friend.

Stephanie Powers
Actress
Interviewed: 2003

I FIRST MET STEPHANIE POWERS one evening in the late 1950s, when we were in pursuit of our careers as young actors in Hollywood. She was actor Peter Brown's date that night, whom I knew very well. Peter and I did our screen tests together at Warner Bros. and we were both signed to studio contracts at that time. We were attending a screening or some sort of social event when we ran into each other. That's when Peter introduced me to Stephanie. She was very pretty; possessed a great smile and had a special presence about her. Stephanie spoke about her gift of language during our interview, "I speak seven languages. I think it's musical and having a musical ear. It's very much a gift." She also shared that, "I'm a great fan of communication through the good use of language." I saw Stephanie several months ago and she looked beautiful, and still has that exceptional, charismatic quality.

I got to know Stephanie very well when she was playing softball with many of the young actresses on the weekends in Hollywood. They had teams that played competitively, but most of all, had an awful lot of fun. Stephanie was one of the better athletes on the field. The actors had an Entertainer's League that was well-organized and highly competitive. The men's league had sponsors that paid for their uniforms and they attended every game. When the actresses played, we went to their games and rooted for certain players. When the actors played, they came to our games, so we all got to know each other very well. Throughout the years when I saw Stephanie, we enjoyed reminiscing about our early days, especially when we were all playing baseball in Hollywood.

Stephanie Powers went on to achieve stardom in motion pictures, television and on the stage.

She appeared in many feature films: *Experiment in Terror, The Interns, McClintock, Die My Darling, Love Has Many Faces, Stagecoach, Herbie Rises Again,* and *The Man Inside,* just to

name a few. Her television series included *The Girl from U.N.C.L.E., The Feather and Father Gang,* and of course, the ever-popular *Hart to Hart.* Regarding *Hart to Hart,* Stephanie said, "How wonderful that you're not only worked making a living doing something you enjoyed, having a great time producing a quality show that you were proud of, but creating a positive influence which I think is a real privilege, the icing on the cake." Powers starred in several mini-series, including *Washington Behind Closed Doors, Deceptions, Mistrials Daughter, At Mother's Request, Burden of Proof and Beryl Markham: A Shadow on The Sun,* which she also produced.

Stephanie has also appeared on stage in many musical productions, including, *Oliver, Annie Get Your Gun, My Fair Lady,* and the London production of *Matador.* She also starred as the legendary Margo Channing in the revival of *Applause,* the musical *All About Eve* during its U.S. tour, showcasing her singing and dancing prowess for American audiences. She was reunited with Robert Wagner in the play *Love Letters* in London's West End, followed by tours of the play in many cities in the U.S. and Canada. The *Hart to Hart* pair later re-created their weekly TV series in eight two-hour movies for NBC-TV and The Family Channel.

Stephanie hosted the well-received seven-part series on personal investing called, *Funding Your Dreams* for the PBS Network and participated as a correspondent for *Mongo Park,* Microsoft's online adventure magazine. She also hosted a 13-part online series for the Romance Classics Network called *Wine Express* for Lifetime Television.

In 1981, Stephanie Powers was one of the founders of the William Holden Wildlife Educational Foundation, a public charity dedicated to the preservation of wild animals in honor of the late William Holden, serving as its president.

Stephanie described the Educational Center during our interview, "The William Holden Wildlife Education Center serves approximately 10,000 students a year, plus local people in the Bush, to allow people to understand and have first-hand experience to know the alternatives and the understanding of 'Why bother?' that involves the need for the animal's preservation." The Center is located near the mouth of the Kenya Safari Club and the Kenya Game Range, started by Holden in the late 1950s, before conservation became a popular issue.

Stephanie lends her name and talent to so many charitable organizations throughout the world, and to the present day. Every time I see her I smile because Stephanie reminds me of the fun we all had together when we were young, as aspiring actors in pursuit of our careers in Hollywood.

Now she's simply pursuing excellence in her life.

Debbie Reynolds
Actress – Entertainer
Interviewed: 1999

THE FIRST TIME I MET ENTERTAINER DEBBIE REYNOLDS was at a celebrity filled birthday party for a very popular actor, Rory Calhoun. It took place at his home in Beverly Hills, California.

Rory and I became good friends during and after a *Desilu Playhouse* show that I co-starred in, with him and Janice Rule entitled, *The Killer Instinct*. We also appeared together in four episodes of the western television series, *The Texan*, shortly thereafter. Rory was highly professional and one of the most unselfish actors I have ever had the pleasure of working with. For example, Rory could have taken a close-up in a scene we were doing together, but instead, he asked the director to give the close-up to me. In acting on film, the close-up shot is the most desired point of view for an actor and he freely shared that opportunity with me, more than once.

I was not married at the time and Debbie was in between marriages. Rory wanted me to meet Debbie, to be her dinner partner that evening. She could not have been nicer as we had a few laughs, a terrific dinner and good conversation for the duration of the evening. Our relationship didn't go further than that night, but I have wonderful memories of that evening.

Debbie starred in more than 30 films, two Broadway shows, two television series and many TV appearances. She also published two memoirs. Her recordings of "Abba Dabba Honeymoon" and "Tammy" sold more than one million copies, which led to her nightclub debut at the Riviera Hotel in Las Vegas in the mid-1960s.

She put together her first nightclub act there. For the next 25 years, Debbie was a headliner on the casino circuit in Reno and Tahoe, in Las Vegas and Atlantic City, to the famed London Palladium, as well as in concert in every major American city, touring on the average of 42 weeks a year.

During our interview Debbie shared that, "I broke my ankle on stage, it was the only time I've ever been injured. Most athletes and dancers live through a lot of injuries. You just go along with it."

In 1973, she took a break from her nightclub appearances to star in the Broadway revival of *Irene,* breaking all previous box-office records for a Broadway musical, after an enormously successful national tour of the show.

Later, Debbie returned to the musical stage with another hit revival, Irving Berlin's *Annie Get Your Gun*. In 1983, she went back to Broadway again to star in the hit musical, *Woman of The Year* and in 1989, she did a national tour of *The Unsinkable Molly Brown*. Debbie told me on the show that the first song she sang was "I Want to be Loved by You." She continued, "At MGM, it was thrilling. I was so joyful, excited, lucky to be a part of that era. I'll never forget it and I'm sorry the young people aren't able to have that today. We don't have that right now, but it will come back."

Debbie's motion pictures included *Singing in The Rain, The Tender Trap, Tammy and The Bachelor, The Pleasure of His Company, The Singing Nun, Divorce American-Style, How The West Was Won* and *The Unsinkable Molly Brown,* for which she was nominated for an Oscar award.

Throughout her career, Debbie won countless awards and honors as an actress, entertainer and for her many humanitarian contributions. She was a lifelong supporter and fundraiser for the Girl Scouts of America and founder/President of The Thalians, a charitable organization which raised millions of dollars for emotionally disturbed children.

Her dream was to one day establish a Hollywood Motion Picture and Television Museum to house her collection of the largest individual collection of Hollywood memorabilia. Later anticipating her eventual retirement from performing, she established the Debbie Reynolds Professional Rehearsal Studios in North Hollywood, California, which has since become one of the entertainment industry's leading rehearsal and professional training studios.

Reynolds had a very disciplined work ethic. She said, "The greatest talents in the world still have to sweat just as hard as the beginners and that you have to, in order to be good, you have to work extremely hard and sweat a lot and even then you might not make it. But that's the only way you're gonna possibly make something wonderful. Work, work, work."

Debbie was so gracious to be a guest on my radio show despite her very busy schedule. At the time of our interview she was rehearsing to perform the *Debbie Reynolds Show* at the McCallum Theater in Palm Desert, California. Debbie could not have been more cooperative and accommodating, breaking away from her preparations for my one-hour show. I will always remember Debbie Reynolds as a stellar actress, an exceptional performer with a bundle of talent and a kind and generous humanitarian. That lovely, vivacious young lady who I met at Rory Calhoun's birthday party would become one of the most beloved entertainers of our time, and truly deserving of a literary standing ovation from me.

Debbie Reynolds passed away one day after her beloved daughter Carrie Fisher died in 2016, at the age of 84.

Andy Robustelli
National Football League – Hall of Fame
Interviewed: 1999

NATIONAL FOOTBALL HALL OF FAMER, Andy Robustelli and I were born and raised in the same hometown on the west side of Stamford, Connecticut. He was about six years older than me, but I remember him when I was a youngster, watching him play for our alma mater, Stamford High School.

Andy was an outstanding player and received a football scholarship to Arnold College in upstate Connecticut. When I was a teenager, we played sports in our home town, with and against each other. We were both enshrined on Stamford High School's Wall of Fame in 1992. The Wall of Fame stands as an inspiration to the students, representing Alumni from all walks of life; show business, sports, politics and other fields, who accomplished great things after graduation.

Andy spent three years in the Navy before he attended and played football as an offensive and defensive end for Arnold College, a small school in Milford, Connecticut. Upon graduation he was a 19th round draft pick by the Los Angeles Rams. Andy revealed, "I was drafted, I think primarily as an offensive player, where you might be more of an advantage to the team rather than to yourself. That's the way it should be, really." The Rams were pretty well set at those positions with Tom Fears and 'Crazy Legs' Hirsch, who both became members of the National Football League Hall of Fame.

It was coach Joe Stydahars' decision to convert Andy to a defensive end. Andy informed us, "More specialized, the start of specialization, probably was the beginning of pro football after the war, and consequently it's grown into a tremendous sport."

He went on to play five years with the Los Angeles Rams and made All Pro two of those years before being traded to the New York Giants. Andy wasn't disappointed over the trade because he was closer to his home in Stamford, Connecticut, just an hour away from Giants Stadium. Andy knew, "You need to play with people that kind of play with each other and

*To Mary Jane and Michael...
With Love and Best Wishes*
Andy Robustelli

CAPTAIN ROBUSTELLI BLITZES THE QUARTERBACK

for each other and you play as a unit. By playing together as a unit, it brings you closer and quicker."

He spent the next nine years molding together a defensive unit that became one of the best in the National Football League's history. His leadership qualities as well as his superior playing abilities, were a big factor for many reasons in the rash of divisional championships the New York Giants enjoyed during the time Andy played there. He said, "You need each other. It makes you a well-rounded player and it makes you understand the game and if you understand the game, you play in a coordinated way."

Andy was exceptionally smart, quick, strong and a superb pass rusher, standing 6'1" and weighing 230 pounds. He recovered twenty-two fumbles and missed only one game in fourteen years. He played on a winning team thirteen of those fourteen years; played in eight NFL title games, seven Pro Bowls, made All-NFL seven years (two with the Rams and five with the New York Giants). He was named NFL's top player of the Maxwell Club of Philadelphia in 1962. He was enshrined in 1971 at Arnold College and The National Football League Hall of Fame in 1971. He indeed, was one of the greatest defensive ends of all time.

After his playing days Andy went on to become a very successful businessman. He was the owner and CEO of the Robustelli World Travel Agency in Stamford, Connecticut. Ironically, Andy didn't like to travel, but he did travel with his wife, to Beverly Hills, California from Stamford, Connecticut to be in my wedding party, in 1992. I know he did it just for me and Mary Jane and I will always be grateful.

We talked on the phone at least once a week for many years, bringing each other up-to-date about what was going on in the entertainment industry, the travel business and with our families.

Mary Jane and I miss him and his wife Jeannie, both deceased now, and their family of nine children and many, many grandchildren and great grandchildren who we spoke about often. I miss hearing and listening to the voice of a fine man, a highly respected sports figure and my best longtime, hometown friend, Andy Robustelli, who passed away in 2011 at the age of 85.

Keely Smith
Singer – Entertainer
Interviewed: 2001

I MET ICONIC JAZZ SINGER AND RECORDING ARTIST Keely Smith in the 1960s at a social event in Hollywood, California. We became friends and remained so for 50 years. My wife Mary Jane and I saw Keely quite often, especially when we both became residents of the Palm Springs, California area. She shared her home, her life and her career with her brother, nicknamed 'Piggy,' who was her road manager, constant companion and best friend. Keely always said he was, "Truly the wind beneath my wings." Piggy and I became close pals; he was very down to earth and fun to be with.

We spent several Christmas Eves with Keely and Piggy, Jerry Vale, Jack Jones and Frankie Randall at the home of Kathleen and Ken Venturis' beautiful home. After we all enjoyed a delicious buffet dinner, we gathered around the piano, with Frankie Randall tickling the ivories, as we all sang Christmas Carols. It was a joy to hear the likes of Keely, Jack, Jerry and Frankie singing solo and then singing duets together. Keely had a unique style and it was such a rare experience to hear her live and up close, singing along with all of those great artists on Christmas Eve. It was magical.

Keely Smith is often referred to as the 'Queen of Swing.' Her charm and artistic honesty, skyrocketed her all the way to the top. The same set of standards applied to both her work and the way she lived; down to earth and totally sincere. She explained how she got her moniker. "I signed a five-CD deal with Concord with the *Swing, Swing, Swing* album. They heard the Sinatra album and wanted that also. That's when I was dubbed the Queen of Swing."

Smith first rose to fame with bandleader Louis Prima, and established her own performing style. The two were married in 1953, and reigned as one of the greatest entertainment teams of all time. "I met Louis in 1948 in Atlantic City. We went out to the pier. I took my baby brother, who I always carried with me. He kept all the servicemen away

from me growing up in Norfolk, because they all thought I was married. Within Louis's big band, the musicians did comedy too. I didn't dance all night. I just sat there and watched the show. We lived together from 1949 to 1953. We were married in '53." Keely added, "That act was Louis Prima. We opened at the Sahara in Las Vegas and the rest of it is almost history."

Keely recorded thirty albums with Prima and another thirty as a solo artist. Her first album recorded in 1957, arranged by Nelson Riddle, produced her signature song, "I Wish You Love," and was nominated for a Grammy Award for best pop female vocalist. That same year, Prima and Smith captured a Grammy for "That Old Black Magic." When Keely debuted as a solo headliner in Las Vegas, the press hailed her as The First Lady of Las Vegas. She told us her thoughts about working with musicians, "I won't work with canned music. I need live musicians. I'm comfortable with them."

Smith toured the country at the finest venues, beginning with the Golden Nugget, the Playboy Hotel in Atlantic City, the Fairmont Hotel in San Francisco and in Chicago, Westbury Music Fair and at the Rainbow Star in New York City. She remembered seeing Aretha Franklin on stage, "Singers were on the stage with Aretha Franklin and they can't even begin to compete with what she does and I'd like to think that she can't compete with what I do, but I bet she could."

As an actress, Keely appeared in the classic *Thunder Road*. She said, "Robert Mitchum, he was gorgeous." And she told us what Robert said about her, "Hey, anybody that can sing a song and interpret the way she does, can act." Keely also appeared in *Hey Boy, Hey Girl* and *The Wildest Show at Tahoe*.

She was seen on numerous television shows with Frank Sinatra, Dean Martin, Perry Como, Dinah Shore, Ed Sullivan, Andy Williams, Joey Bishop, Glen Campbell and the list goes on. Smith spoke about Sinatra, "Frank always called me 'Injun.' We recorded *Keely Sings Sinatra* on his birthday and then he passed away. I stopped production on it." At the time of our interview Keely was working on a feature-length movie, *The Life Story of Louis and Keely*, writing her autobiography and the release of her albums, *Swing, Swing, Swing* and *Keely Sings Sinatra*.

When Keely and I first became friends, she shared with me that she was half-Native American, something she was very proud of. This was many years before I played the title role in the film *Winterhawk,* in 1976. After filming, Keely said she had a renewed and special place in her heart for me and our friendship.

Keely, my dear friend, may the Great Spirit keep you under his wings, from the day you left us at age 89 in 2017, for all eternity.

Elke Sommer
Actress
Interviewed: 1996

I MET VIVACIOUS ACTRESS ELKE SOMMER when she was married to her first husband, Hollywood columnist and author Joe Hyams. We got together for an afternoon of tennis at director Daniel Mann's tennis court in Malibu, California. One of Danny's neighbors was our fourth player and we all enjoyed a couple of sets of mixed doubles matches.

Our friendship continued when she and her husband invited me to play at their tennis court in Bel Air, California. Elke was not only beautiful, but a very talented actress. She was also an outstanding athlete with a wonderful energetic personality. Elke and I were both invited to many celebrity tennis tournaments and celebrity golf tournaments to raise money for various charitable organizations. Through the years, she was one of the best actresses to play the game of golf; if not the best! Elke won many of the tournaments she participated in, including the Frank Sinatra Celebrity Golf Invitational several times. Mary Jane and I still see Elke and her husband, hotelier, Wolf Walther, from time to time. We enjoy talking about all the fun times we shared at charitable and social events.

Elke Sommer, an actress, artist, singer, and stage director, has starred in more than sixty films and several mini-series for television. She shared two very special moments with us from her show business career, "I was discovered by pure accident, by (Italian director) Vittorio De Sica. My absolute idol was Gary Cooper. I met him shortly before he died."

In addition to her work in films, Sommer has guest-starred in numerous episodic television shows, performed on stage in the United States and abroad, as well as having directed many stage productions.

She also recorded best-selling albums in four of the five fluid languages she speaks, and set house records in America and Europe for her roles in the theater.

Her critically acclaimed artwork has been featured in shows in major galleries around the world. She hosted a series, *Painting with Elke* on national television and also authored a

book on the subject. "I knew a little bit that I had joy. I would paint more than the other kids. To perfect your style, you have to be very disciplined; to find your own style so when people see your paintings, it's recognizable." But sometimes the opposite situation happened. Elke divulged, "I'll have an exhibition and I'll sign E. Schwartz on all the paintings so people won't know they are my paintings to just buy them for a high-priced autograph just because it was my art. At the end of the exhibition, the gallery owner told everyone that bought them knew that they were, in fact, done by Elke Sommer."

Sports Illustrated magazine dubbed her one of the best lady tennis and golf players on the celebrity circuit. She asked the question, "Is it true that the name GOLF is Gentlemen Only Ladies Forbidden? I heard that and it was the funniest thing." Elke is also a prize-winning race car driver and hosted the nationally syndicated television show, *The World of Speed and Beauty*. "When I was in my early twenties, I always like cars and I had a great favor for fast cars in Europe. I had no fear; that is, of course, very good." About the show, Elke said, "It was very exciting. It involved every kind of speed and beauty of the machine; every kind. I rode in everything except the motorcycles. There I wanted to drive formula, which I hadn't driven yet. A formula, you sit in the middle. Once you get fear, you can't do it anymore. We should listen to our inner voice many times in life."

She has worked with some of the top male stars in the movie business; with Oliver Reed in *Severed Ties* and *The Prisoner of Zenda* with Peter Sellers. "Peter was very complex and generous with his time and talent. He asked me to marry him."

Elke also appeared in, *Zeppelin* with Michael York, *The Invincible Six* with Curt Jurgens, *The Wrecking Crew* with Dean Martin, *The Money Trap* with Glenn Ford, *The Art of Love* with James Garner, *The Heroes of Telemark* with Kirk Douglas and *The Prize* with Paul Newman. Elke shared with us, "Paul became a very good buddy."

Some of the stage plays Elke has appeared in are *Born Yesterday*, *Same Time Next Year*, *Woman of The Year*, *Cactus Flower*, *California Suite*, *Irma La duce*, and more. Her point of view about her devoted fans was, "People are people. Your audiences adore you and its a good experience and you get a great ovation, and you make them laugh."

Elke's stellar career has been rich with achievements and accolades and she continues to see new challenges with a humble approach. In spite of all that she has accomplished, Elke is confident, "The best is yet to come."

Rod Steiger
Actor
Interviewed: 2000

I met Academy Award-winning actor, Rod Steiger in 1959 when we worked together in the film *Seven Thieves* at 20th Century Fox Studios. We had an excellent cast that included Edward G. Robinson, Rod Steiger, Joan Collins, Eli Wallach, Alexander Scourby, Berry Kroeger and me, which comprised the seven thieves that robbed the Casino in Monte Carlo. This was the first of a five-picture contract I had with 20th Century Fox. It was a pleasure to be working with such fine actors in an excellent caper written and produced by Sydney Boehm, and directed by one of Hollywood's finest, Henry Hathaway. Many of my scenes were with Rod Steiger, and it was interesting and exciting from beginning to end to be working with him. Rod and I became fast friends and on several occasions he invited me for dinner at his beach house in Malibu, California. Rod was a generous, gracious host and always had some interesting, talented people at these get-togethers who had lots of show business stories to tell.

Steiger won an Academy Award for best actor for his fine performance in *In the Heat of the Night*, nominated for best actor in *The Pawnbroker* and best supporting actor in *On the Waterfront*. Rod told us, "The success of *Waterfront* saved me years of looking for a job. I was very lucky." He also won the Golden Globe Award, British Academy Award, National Society of Film Critics Award and New York Film Critics Award for Best Actor, in the 1967 film, *In the Heat of the Night*. Rod said about playing the character of Chief Gillespie, chewing gum, in *In the Heat of the Night*, "If you take something you don't like or think is impossible artistically and accept it as a challenge, rather than a reproach, what happened was I found out that I could communicate what I was actually thinking by how he chewed. There's a way sometimes to take a cliché and make it your own."

Rod was a Golden Globe Award nominee for best actor in *The Pawnbroker*, won the British Academy Award for best foreign actor for *The Pawnbroker* and won the Italian

Academy Award for Best Actor in *The Sergeant*. Rod said about *The Pawnbroker*, "I found out emotionally how to do the part rather than intellectually. That's funny, you never know when you get into acting what's gonna help you."

Steiger has portrayed larger-than-life characters, more than any other actor that I know. He's portrayed Rasputin, Steinmetz, Pontius Pilate, Andrei Vishinsky, Richard Burbage, Rudolf Hess, Ulysses S. Grant, Benito Mussolini, Sam Giancanna, Robert E. Peary and Al Capone. However, it was his portrayal of the uneventful life of a hard-luck butcher, written by Paddy Chayefsky entitled, *Marty,* that launched his movie career.

Some of his other films were *Oklahoma, The Big Knife, The Harder They Fall, Cry Terror, Doctor Zhivago, The Illustrated Man, Lucky Luciano, W.C. Fields and Me, The Amityville Horror, Lion of the Desert, The Chosen*, and, of course, the movie we did together with Eddie G. Robinson and Joan Collins entitled, *Seven Thieves*. Rod smiled and said, "I'll always remember you on the side of the building." I answered him, "To me, that's improv! I didn't come out on the ledge, I refused, which made you come back in, to pull me onto that ledge. We improvised that whole scene; it was all our work." Rod's more recent films were *The Hurricane, End of Days, Crazy in Alabama, The Flying Dutchman,* and *The Hollywood Sign.*

In addition to Hathaway and Chayefsky, Steiger worked with some of the great writers and directors during his illustrious career, such as Norman Jewison, John Frankenheimer, Arthur Miller, David Lean, Elia Kazan, Tim Burton, and Sidney Lumet.

He received twelve lifetime achievement awards, including The International Humanitarian Gift of Life, Inc. Award, Man of the Year Award from Interval House Crisis Shelter and received his star on Hollywood Walk of Fame in 1997.

The day we went to Rod's home to record the interview, he picked me up, swung me around and said how happy he was to see me. The feeling was mutual. I'll never forget the comradery we had; we were like brothers. The last words he ever spoke to me before we left were, "When are we going to do the next one?" Rod Steiger took his final bow two years later, in 2002, at the age of 77.

Steiger left us with these words of wisdom from someone who knew all too well, "They can teach you anything but they can't teach you talent. If you don't have that type of imagination, you can go to school for four hundred years, nothing's gonna happen. Nothing new will happen."

50

Connie Stevens

Actress

Interviewed: 1995

THE FIRST TIME I MET CONNIE STEVENS was at Warner Bros. Studios in the late 1950s when we were both under contract to the studio. She was the studio darling and a very popular young actress. At the time she was co-starring with Robert Conrad in the successful television series, *Hawaiian Eye.*

Connie and I did a lot of motion picture and television magazine layouts. They were vital for promoting young actors with star potential and we did them because we were under contract to the various major studios. We became friends as a result and I had the pleasure of meeting her loving, talented family. I was treated like a member of the family whenever I was invited for lunch or dinner at their home. They were the nicest, most gracious people you could ever meet. I always get a smile on my face when I think of the times I spent with Connie and her family. It was the beginning of a lifelong friendship, which continues to this day.

Connie has starred in films, television, Broadway, recordings and the concert stage. She gained worldwide popularity and recognition as a multi-talented performer and businesswoman. Connie has performed for presidents at the White House and overseas for soldiers in Vietnam and Persian Gulf.

It all began with her musical artistry at the age of sixteen with a singing group called The Three Debs. She later joined three male vocalists known as the Fourmost. The Three Debs, Connie said, "I'm sure they're still singing because they were very, very gifted singers. I learned a lot from them."

The Fourmost, she said, "The Fourmost became the Lettermen. Then I was discovered for the movies. They went on to become the Lettermen and I went on to be myself." She recorded as a soloist, as the very first artist on the newly formed Warner Brothers label. She recorded a big hit single "Kookie, Kookie, Lend Me Your Comb," a duet with Edd 'Kookie'

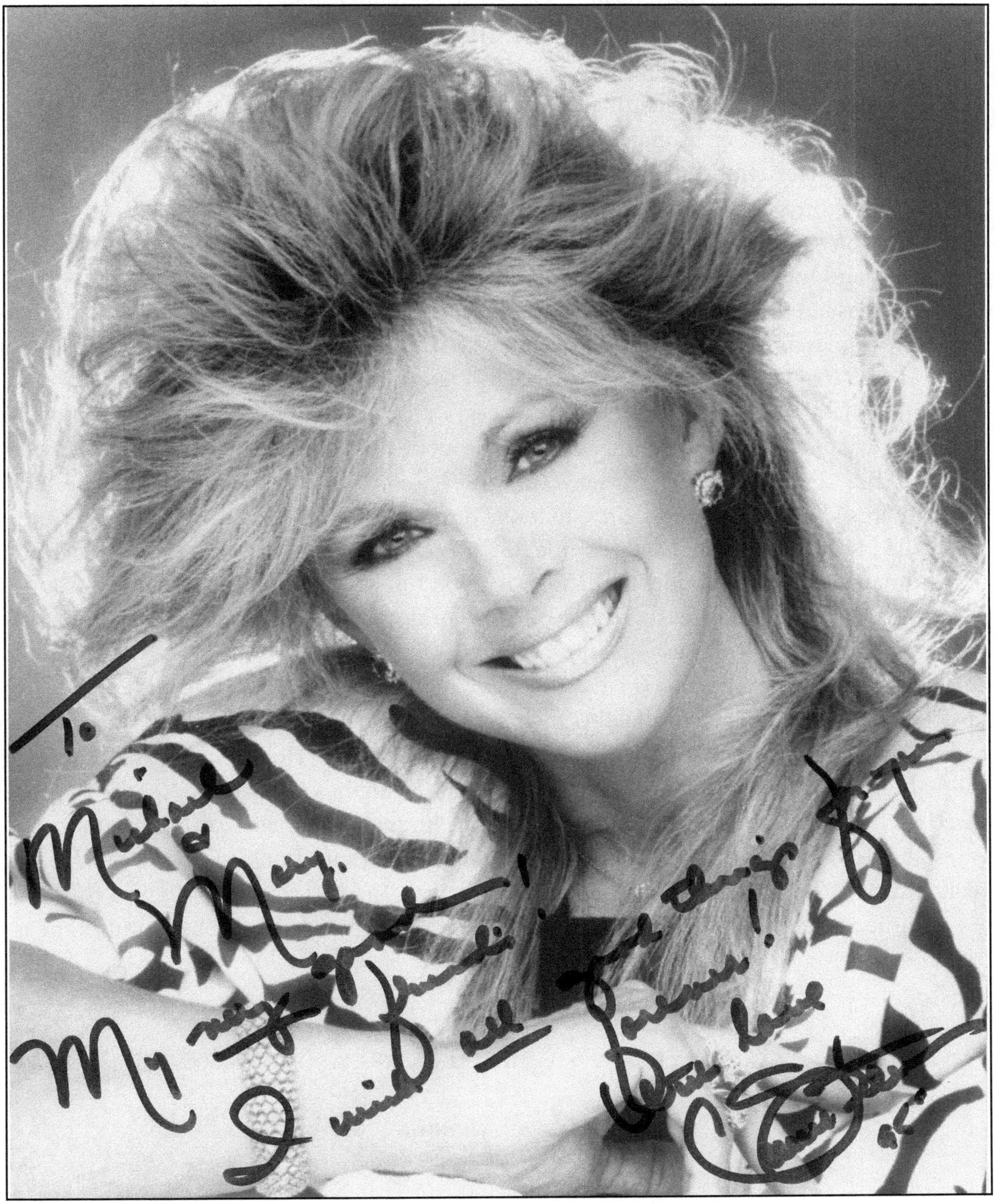

Connie Stevens

Byrnes. It was the No. 4 record in the country in spring 1959.

Connie went on to record a beautiful Christmas album called, *Tradition*. On it she sang with her two talented daughters, Joely and Tricia, which was released on the GTS label. Prior to the making of this album, Connie recorded an original Christmas single written by songwriter Carol Connors entitled, "Every Day Should be Christmas." All the proceeds from the record sales were donated to Children's Hospitals.

She began her acting career in the 1950s, with her endearing role as Cricket Blake in the hit television series, *Hawaiian Eye*. Several motion pictures followed, *Parrish, Susan Slade, Drag Strip* and *Never Too Late*. There was also *The Grissom Gang, Greece Two, Back to The Beach*, and the fun, box-office hit *Palm Springs Weekend*. Connie also starred opposite George Burns in the popular TV series, *Wendy and Me*. She appeared in several other series, telefilms, miniseries, and movies of the week, including *Starting from Scratch, Scruples, Bring Me the Head of Dobie Gillis, Murder She Wrote, The Love Boat* and more.

Connie has experienced phenomenal success in the business world, having created one of the most talked about cosmetic skin care product lines in the industry called Forever Spring. "The concept was my garden," Connie shared. "Another chance to blossom and grow. There's always one more chance to look your best." Connie also debuted her perfume line, called Kali, for women. "My perfume line called Kali, an exotic floral. I call it the 'heart of a woman.' Kali was a goddess. The idea is to be full and rounded as a female." Connie continued, "It's sort of a catalyst. When you look good and you feel good about yourself, and you accomplish a lot of things you set out to do."

This vivacious and generous lady spends a great deal of her free time with one of her favorite charities, Project Windfeather, helping the mentally and physically disadvantaged to become working members of the community in Jackson Hole, Wyoming. "They are trained for whatever their aptitude is. Every human being has that special 'spark.' They are cared for by the community." Connie added her feelings about others in the community she cares about, too. "The Native Americans should be a treasure to us and not a burden. It's really time to help all Americans and be one."

Connie Stevens' most endearing quality is her charm, as special and beautiful as she is.

George Takei
Actor
Interviewed: 2002

I MET GEORGE TAKEI IN 1967 when I guest-starred with Julie Newmar in the original *Star Trek* series segment, "Friday's Child." He enjoyed our show for many reasons; the cast, the director, Joseph Pevney, the crew and location. George liked the script because it had several dimensions of action, drama, suspense and comedy, all in a one-hour show.

"*Star Trek* made an absolute impact and certainly a career changing impact on my life," George shared during our interview on my radio show. He added, "In addition, I was a big fan of the show and had a great deal of respect for talented Mr. Gene Roddenberry, the creator of *Star Trek*. I am deeply indebted to Mr. Roddenberry for having the good judgement, intelligence and taste to cast me as Mr. Sulu."

Takei was not in any of the scenes with me and Julie Newmar because he was back at the ship, The Enterprise, during this episode. Most of our scenes were with Captain Kirk, portrayed by William Shatner, Mr. Spock played by Leonard Nimoy and De Forest Kelley who was Dr. McCoy. George and I met and talked briefly when we did some of the interior scenes for the show back at Paramount Studios in Hollywood. Years later we were both cast in a movie that was made in the Philippines, *Return from The River Kwai*. It was produced by Kurt Unger and directed by Andrew Mc Laglen. George played a sadistic Japanese commanding officer of a prison camp during World War II. It certainly was a departure from his work in *Star Trek* and his characterization was very convincing; he did an outstanding job.

During the interview George elaborated, "*Star Trek* opened my casting opportunities globally." For the second time, we didn't work in any of the scenes together because in this film I played the commander of the submarine that took place in sequences that George was not in.

The cast and crew all stayed at that the same hotel in Makati in the Philippines, and we socialized in the evenings when we had a day off.

It was many years later that George and I got to know each other better when we appeared at several *Star Trek* conventions in Los Angeles. George was very popular at all of the conventions in and out of the country, as well as all of the other cast members. Loyal *Star Trek* fans always showed up in droves and were eager to purchase all of the memorabilia the cast had to offer. Throughout the years and until this day, the actors continue to make more money at these venues than they did when they were on the show!

George's acting debut occurred on live television in the drama series, *Playhouse 90*. His motion picture debut was in *The Ice Palace* starring Richard Burton. His other films include six *Star Trek* motion pictures, *Kissinger and Nixon*, *Prisoners of The Sun*, *The Green Berets*, *Walk Don't Run*, *An American Dream*, *PT 109*, *Majority of One*, *Hell to Eternity*, and *Return from The River Kwai*.

Some of his television appearances include *Mission Impossible*, *Twilight Zone*, *Perry Mason*, *Hallmark Hall of Fame*, *Miami Vice*, *I Spy*, *Marcus Welby, M.D.*, *Hawaiian Eye*, *Hawaii Five-0*, *The Six Million Dollar Man*, *Voyage to The Bottom of the Sea*, *The Wackiest Ship in the Army*, *Death Valley Days*, *Baa Baa Black Sheep*, *Chico and the Man*, *The Courtship of Eddie's Father*, *MacGyver*, *My Three Sons*, *Murder She Wrote*, and many others.

George's theatrical credits include *Undertow*, *The Wash*, *Year of the Dragon*, *Fly Blackbird*, a musical version of *Snow White*, and was the genie in *Aladdin* at the Hexagon Theater in Redding, England. George said, "I went to school in England as a young lad and I made it a point to go every year to London on my theater-going rounds. Actors are actors all over. The British are more technically trained and Americans are more internal and introspective in their approach. The British audience is much more deeply grounded in the theater tradition because every small provincial village has their theater. They are trained from an early age to go to the theater and get the joy of that communal experience."

Among his credits is a music industry accolade, a 1987 Grammy nomination in the Best-Spoken Word or Non-Musical Recording category. George's distinctive voice is featured in Walt Disney Pictures' full-length animated feature *Mulan*, in *Star Trek* audio novel recordings, Fox Television's *The Simpsons*, *Futurama*, and numerous voice-overs and narrations.

Takei's talents also extend to writing. He wrote a science-fiction novel entitled, *Mirror Friend, Mirror Foe*. As told in his autobiography, *To the Stars*, George and his family were placed in a United States internment camp at outbreak of World War II. George spent most of his childhood at Camp Roher in the swamps of Arkansas and at wind-swept Camp Tule Lake in northern California.

George and his family eventually returned to his native Los Angeles, which shaped his acting career. Graduating from Los Angeles High School, George enrolled in the University of California at Berkeley. He later transferred to the University of California at Los Angeles, where he received a Bachelor of Arts in Theater in 1960 and a Master of Arts in Theater in 1964. He attended the Shakespeare Institute at Stratford-Upon-Avon in England and Sofia University in Tokyo, Japan. In Hollywood, George later studied acting at the Desilu Workshop. It didn't take long for his star to shine and enjoy the fruits of success as an actor and author.

George is busier than ever these days. He is the Chairman of the Board of the Japanese American National Museum in the Little Tokyo area of downtown Los Angeles, California. His *Star Trek* uniform is proudly displayed in one of the museum's exhibits.

It has been a pleasure getting to know George Takei over the years.

Constance Towers
Actress – Singer
Interviewed: 1999

I met actress, singer Constance Towers in 1964 when we were starring together in one of director Sammy Fuller's *The Naked Kiss*. Constance was superb and I thought she should have been nominated for a best actress award. Constance and I were both perfectly cast in the film. She was the consummate professional and very easy to work with and we had an onscreen compatibility that made the story even more compelling.

I didn't see Constance for many years after we finished the movie, as we were both still working in the film industry, but on different productions. Eventually, I contacted Constance and asked her to be a guest on my radio show. She invited my wife, Mary Jane and I to her home in Los Angeles to record the interview. We met her husband, handsome actor and U.S. Ambassador to Mexico, John Gavin. Mary Jane did an excellent job as my engineer and co-producer of the show. We work very well together as a team.

Constance was born in one of my favorite towns, Whitefish, Montana. It is about 20 miles down the road from Kalispell, Montana, where we filmed *Winterhawk*. I also had the honor of being the Grand Marshal at the Whitefish Winter Festival, that they celebrated every year.

Constance began her theatrical career as a singer, and made nightclub appearances in the Persian Room of New York's Plaza Hotel and the New York St. Regis' Maisonette. Next, on to Broadway where she starred in the Lincoln Center Production of *Showboat*, the musical *Ari*, an adaptation of the Leon Uris novel *Exodus*, Anna with Yul Bryner in T*he King and I*, Stephen Sondheim's *Follies*, *The Sound of Music*, *42nd St.*, *Oklahoma*, *Camelot*, *Mame*, *Cactus Flower* and Chicago's 1989 stage production of *Steel Magnolias*.

Her work has received critical acclaim. Constance has been honored as the recipient of the New York Critics Outer Circle Award for Excellence in Theater, The American Academy of Dramatic Arts Achievement Award and the Best Actress of 1974 Award by the New

Jersey Drama Critics Association.

Towers made the transition to Hollywood and has appeared on numerous episodic television shows, *The Rockford Files, Fantasy Island, Midnight Caller, Designing Women, Home Shopping Club, High Society, Frazier, Caroline in the City, On Wings of Eagles* and received an Emmy Award nomination for her fine performance in the CBS television network special, *Once in Her Life*. She played the villainess, Helena Cassadine on the daytime soap opera *General Hospital*. Constance revealed, "Elizabeth Taylor originally created the role in the early 1980s, who is richer and more powerful. It's the first time I've played a role like that. It's great fun and a wonderful challenge." Constance was the mysterious Juliana Deschanel on the daytime soap *Sunset Beach* and played Clarissa McCandless on the CBS soap *Capitol*.

Constance made her motion picture debut opposite John Wayne and William Holden in John Ford's, *The Horse Soldiers* and another Ford Western, *Sergeant Rutledge*. Constance spoke about John Wayne, "He really was what you wanted him to be and dealt with life and people in such an open and honest way. He was a man who stood on his own." She also shared memories of working on the set with director John Ford, "He played such incredible tricks on you and on everybody else, but that was part of the fun of John Ford," Her other films include *Fate is The Hunter, Shock Corridor*, another film by Sammy Fuller, *Fast Forward, Karate Kid 4, The Relic, A Perfect Murder* and of course, *The Naked Kiss*." Constance remembered Sammy Fuller in *The Naked Kiss*, "How sensitive and dear he was with the children. Sammy was rather child-like himself. Part of his charm and part of his talent was being totally uninhibited himself. He was quite an extraordinary character. He had ideas and wasn't afraid to use them."

I was fortunate to have starred with Constance Towers and our work together with famed director Sammy Fuller in *The Naked Kiss* was one of the best professional experiences of my life. It has been called one of the greatest film noir movies of all time.

After working with him, I knew how much Sammy loved actors; he loved to listen. Director Martin Scorsese said the opening sequence of *The Naked Kiss* was his favorite and one of the best opening sequences of any picture of all time. Constance told us that it was the first time the hand held camera was used for that sequence, and added, "I think the greatest compliment to Sammy Fuller is that John Ford would come every afternoon and have tea. He loved to watch Sammy work. Probably the greatest compliment a director would have because John Ford was considered by all directors the great, great director, cinematographer and understood the poetry of films so well. He loved Sammy."

I am so grateful Constance became my friend. I often think about our extraordinary experience working with Sammy Fuller in *The Naked Kiss* and how special it will always be for both of us.

Jerry Vale
Singer – Recording Artist
Interviewed: 1995

I MET SINGER, RECORDING ARTIST JERRY VALE many years ago at one of our Lunch Bunch gatherings at the ever-popular celebrity hangout, Café Roma Restaurant in Beverly Hills, California. I got acquainted with all the interesting personalities, who were all part of show business, but Jerry had been on the road working at a singing engagement when I joined the group in the 1980s. Upon his return, we were introduced and our friendship grew steadily from that day forward. Shortly thereafter, my wife Mary Jane and I met Jerry's wife Rita and soon we all became very close friends.

Jerry and I had much in common; we loved sports, especially baseball and golf. Throughout the years we participated in many celebrity charity golf tournaments to raise money throughout the greater Los Angeles area. As time passed, we both moved from Los Angeles to the Palm Springs area. We saw each other quite often and spent many holidays together. We participated in countless celebrity charity golf tournaments, including my celebrity golf tournament for eight years. We were like family.

Jerry Vale began singing at the age of twelve in his native Bronx, New York. Jerry shared, "My mother had a beautiful singing voice. When we used to get together on Sundays at my grandmother's house, everybody would get up and sing. I used to look forward to that. That's where I really got my love for singing."

It wasn't long before he signed a recording contract with Columbia Records and was singing in all the world's most prestigious resorts, theaters and cabarets.

Jerry explained, "I recorded only for Columbia Records. I was 20 years old when I signed that contract. My first record was, 'And No One Knows.' And no one knew it, either!" He added, "Today, if a record comes out and it doesn't make it in three or four days, it's gone. When we would make a record, if it came out and wasn't a hit immediately, they (the recording company) would stay with it. They wouldn't just throw it away."

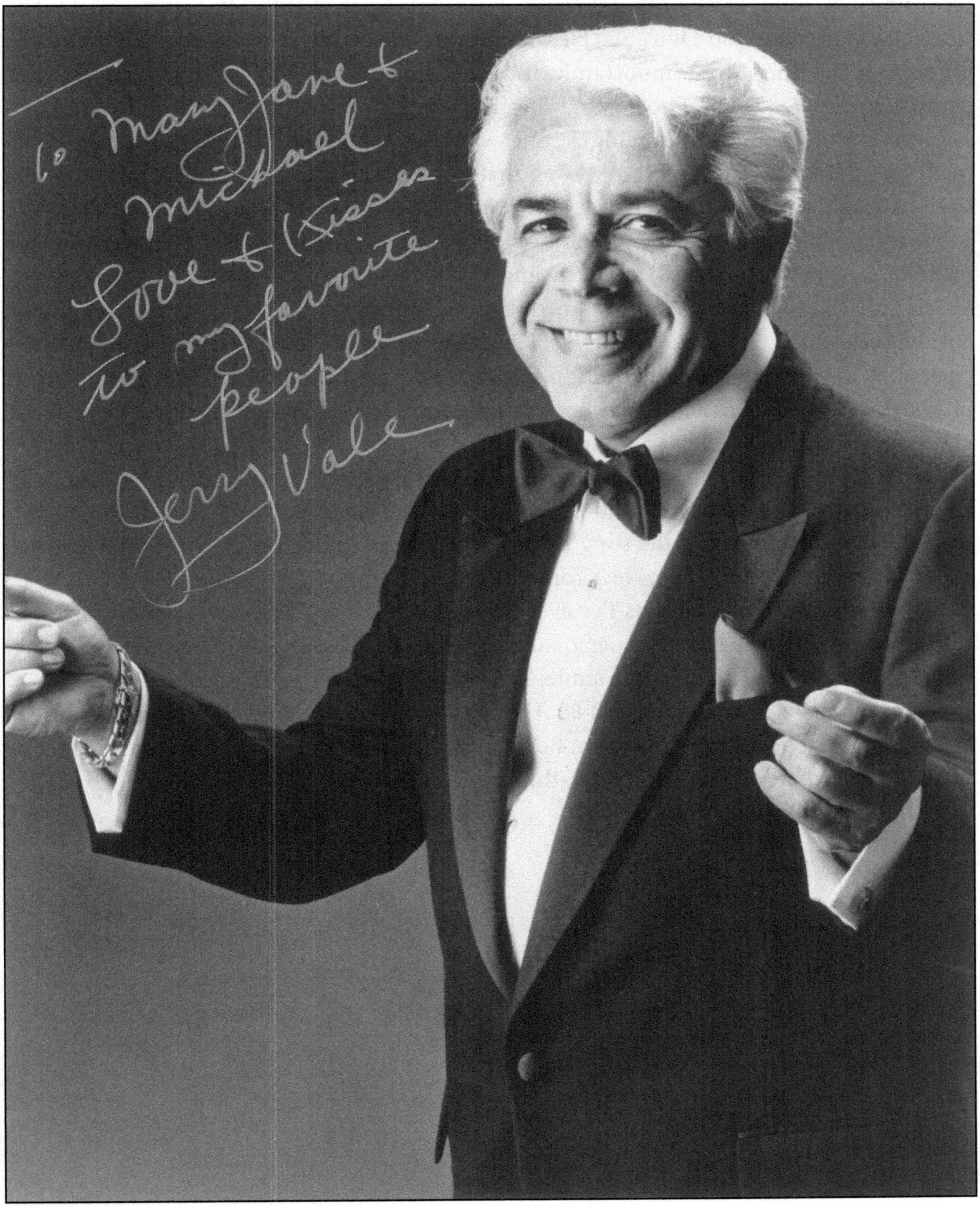
To Mary Jane &
Michael
Love & Kisses
to my favorite
people
Jerry Vale

He became known as the Ambassador of Song for contemporary romantic music. Jerry's recordings of, "And This is My Beloved," "Have You Looked into My Heart," "Al-Di-La," "Camelot," "Pretend You Don't See Her, Mama," and "You Don't Know Me," have all been hit records for him. More importantly, these songs have become standards, for all time, because of his unique vocal power and sincerity.

Jerry's attitude towards singing a song was a personal one. "I don't think you could really put the kind of feeling into a song that you have to make believable, unless you've lived part of it, you know? Whenever you're singing a song you're acting, I guess. When I do a love song, I'm acting it out. My favorite album, I would have to say is, *I Remember Buddy*. I think I sang better on that than I ever sang in my life."

Jerry parlayed his singing into appearing on numerous television variety and talk shows, episodic television and motion pictures. His engagement at Carnegie Hall playing before a packed house led to a standing ovation for his stellar performance. He appeared in a pair of Martin Scorsese's classics: the award-winning film, *Goodfellas* and *Casino*. The Scorsese family was a big fan of Jerry Vale and his music.

Jerry loved baseball and was a big New York Yankees fan. His recording of "The Star-Spangled Banner" was played by more than eleven baseball teams during several consecutive seasons. His gold record of the song is the only such recording on display at the Baseball Hall of Fame in Cooperstown, New York.

Of all the Christmas albums I've ever heard, I think Jerry Vale's *A Personal Christmas Collection* is by far the best. His personal favorite on the album was "Santa Mouse." Every time I hear that song, it makes me smile, knowing that Jerry loved it, too.

Jerry left us in 2014 at the age of 83. He was like a brother to me and I miss his sense of humor, loyal friendship and the talent he left behind. There will always be a Jerry Vale song playing somewhere, at any given time, throughout the world.

And that's the greatest gift of all.

Mamie Van Doren
Actress
Interviewed: 2008

I MET MAMIE VAN DOREN in the late 1950s when I was under contract to Warner Bros. Studios. She was starring in a contemporary western film entitled, *Born Reckless* co-starring with Jeff Richards, Arthur Hunnicutt, Carol Ohmart and directed by Howard W. Koch. I had a small part in the film, playing a cowboy in a dancing sequence with Mamie. It was very early in my career and it was the first time I danced in a movie. The film was the beginning of our friendship, which continues to this day.

I must say I enjoyed myself immensely working with Mamie Van Doren; she had a great sense of humor and we had a bundle of laughs filming our sequence. Mamie was beautiful, with an outgoing personality and a gorgeous figure. Mamie told me and our listening audience with a smile, "I'm part Swedish and part Sioux. On the other side is Scottish, Irish and Dutch. A little Sioux got in there. I never talk about this; nobody ever asks me."

Van Doren appeared in approximately forty-one motion pictures beginning with *Jet Pilot* with John Wayne, *Two Tickets to Broadway, His Kind of Woman* with Robert Mitchum and Jane Russell, *Yankee Pasha* with Jeff Chandler and Rhonda Fleming, *Francis Joins the Wacs, Ain't Misbehavin', Running Wild, Star in The Dust, Untamed Youth, Teacher's Pet* with Clark Gable, *High School Confidential, The Private Lives of Adam and Eve,* and the list goes on. Mamie shared about her beginnings in films, "In *Jet Pilot* with John Wayne, Howard Hughes discovered me in Palm Springs when I was in a beauty contest. That's how I got my contract with RKO. I was still in high school and he flew me to Las Vegas, signed me for five or six pictures and that's when I did *Jet Pilot*."

About working with Clark Gable in *Teacher's Pet*, Mamie said, "He was a man's man. I played opposite him; he was my boyfriend. He was in his fifties and I was twenty-four, twenty-five and it didn't bother me at all. I loved him. I was crazy about him."

Mamie's television appearances were many, including *Ozzie and Harriet, The Jack Benny Show, The Real McCoys*, appeared regularly on *The Tonight Show starring Johnny Carson, The Steve Allen Show, The Red Skelton Show, The Merv Griffin Show, Joey Bishop, Entertainment Tonight, Hard Copy, The Larry King Show, Good Morning America* and many more.

Mamie knew Marilyn Monroe and liked her. "I liked Marilyn. We hit it off right away. We got along well. I had a screen test at 20th Century Fox. I was really upset because I didn't think I would get in there. She had gone through the same thing. She was very introverted; a thinker, but she wasn't stupid. Marilyn told me, "There's other studios. Just keep taking it." She knew how I was feeling because she had gone through the same things. I was kinda shy, more than she was."

Her nightclub appearances were with the top entertainment venues in the USA at the Sands Hotel with Sammy Davis Jr., Thunderbird, Riviera, and El Rancho Hotel, all in Las Vegas. She also performed at the Latin Quarter in New York City with the great Jackie Gleason. Mamie's international popularity extended to Mexico, Brazil, Argentina, France, Italy, Holland and Brussels. She was honored at the Palm Springs Film Noir Film Festival, showcasing her movie, *Guns, Girls and Gangster* and received a sidewalk star in Hollywood, California on the Hollywood Walk of Fame in 1994.

Writer Barry Lowe wrote *The Atomic Blonde* about her and MacFarland published the book. Mamie was pleased with the outcome and commented about it, "He thought I should be acknowledged for my work rather than for just the way I look. It got great reviews and I'm so excited that people acknowledge my work."

We have remained friends with Mamie and her husband, Thomas and Mary Jane and I occasionally meet them in Newport Beach, in Southern California, to share a meal and talk about Hollywood, working together in *Born Reckless,* and our careers. Mamie is a love, on and off the screen. She lit up the set and brought the scenes to life with her energy, beauty and talent.

Today, she lights up our lives.

Ken Venturi
Professional Golf Association — Golf Hall of Fame
Interviewed: 2004

I met Ken Venturi and his lovely wife Kathleen at Buddy Greco's Supper Club in Cathedral City, California about 15 years ago. My wife Mary Jane and I were joining our friends Jerry and Rita Vale, who had invited Ken and Kathleen, as well. We were introduced that night and became friends from that moment on.

I invited Ken to our Lunch Bunch gathering in the Palm Springs area. Ken was an instant hit with everyone, sharing his wonderful stories when he was a pro golfer and later the many years that he was an analyst for CBS, covering the PGA Tour. His sincerity and straightforwardness about the stories he told, was most appreciated by everyone. Ken was one of the most honest, sincere human beings I had ever met.

Mary Jane and I had the pleasure of spending a number of Christmas Eve dinner parties at Ken and Kathleen's beautiful home. They were always joyful, festive gatherings that usually included Jerry and Rita Vale, Keely Smith, Jack Jones, Frankie Randall and Buddy Greco, plus family and friends. The food, atmosphere and love that transcended was always a special Christmas Eve for all of us. Christmas Carols, sung by many of the talented singers there, was the topper of the evening.

Ken Venturi was one of the most outstanding Professional Golf Association players to ever play on the tour. He became a professional in 1956 and joined the tour in 1957. In his first year he won the St. Paul Open and the Miller Open. In 1958, he won the Thunderbird Invitational, Phoenix Open, Baton Rouge Open, Los Angeles Open and the Glen Eagle Chicago Open in 1958 and 1959.

Ken told me that, "I was known as a very cocky young man because I gave very short answers because I was a very bad stutterer. I told my mom that I was going to pick the

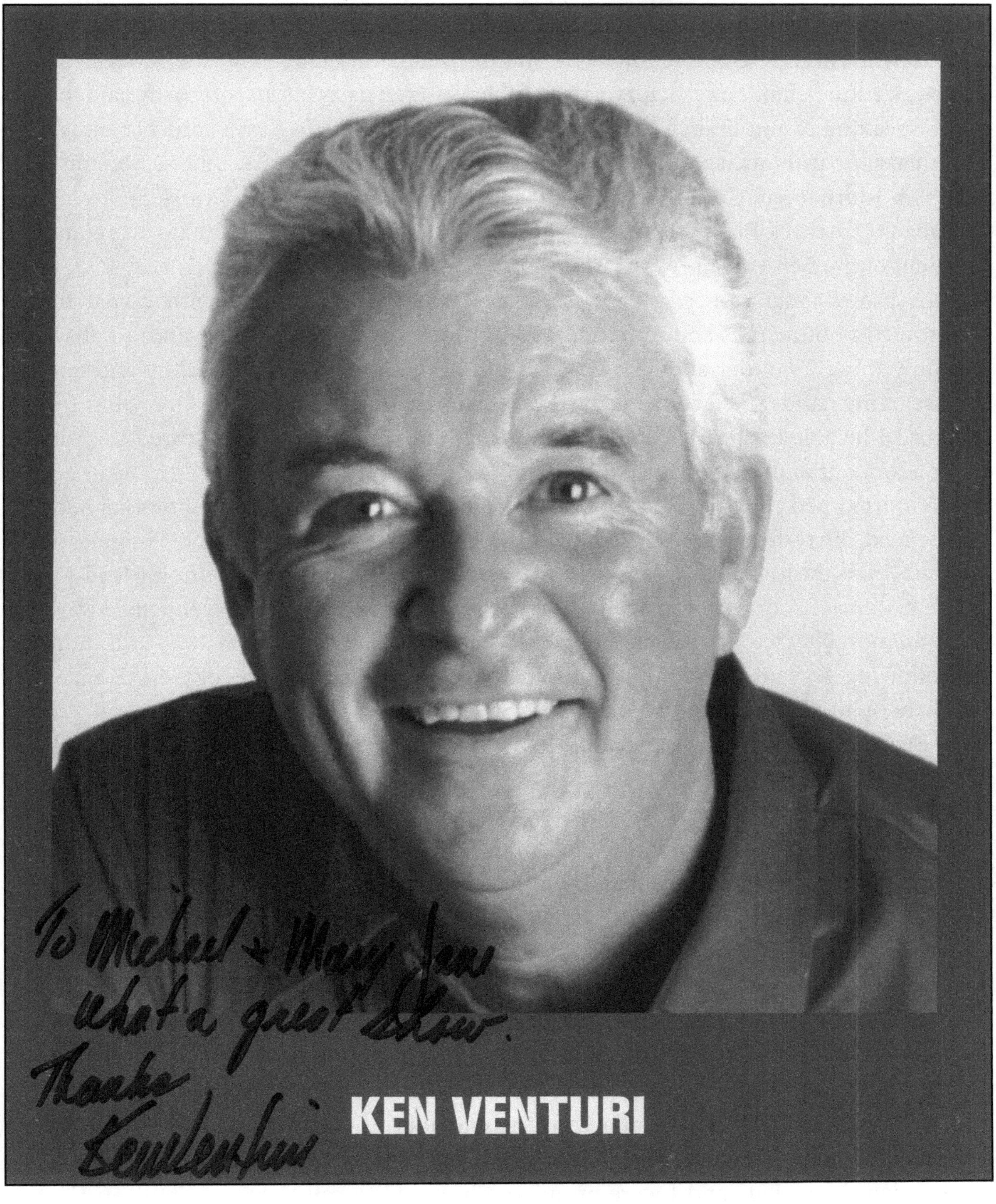
To Michael + Mary Jane
what a great show.
Thanks
Ken Venturi
KEN VENTURI

loneliest sport. I got into it and it was nothing to practice eight hours a day, just to be by myself."

He captured the Bing Crosby National and Milwaukee Open in 1960. In 1964, he came back to win The U.S. Open followed by The Insurance City Open and the American Golf Classic. Venturi's final tour victory came at the San Francisco Lucky International Open in 1966. Speaking of San Francisco, there is a dedication plaque to Ken Venturi in one of the Terminals at San Francisco International Airport. In previous years, he was a member of the PGA Tournament Committee, PGA Player of The Year, *Sports Illustrated* Sportsman of The Year, Comeback Player of The Year in 1964, a member of the Ryder Cup Team and the recipient of the Ben Hogan Award in 1965.

His professional career was cut short when he was diagnosed with carpal tunnel syndrome in both wrists and retired in 1967. "I was only on tour for ten-and-a-half-years. The only thing I wonder about is what I could have done if I stayed healthy and not lost the use of my hands." Ken continued, "I was fortunate though to win the Open, but I never dreamt I'd be able to speak, let alone think I'd go into television. I was scared to death I'd make a fool out of myself on air."

Venturi joined CBS sports in 1968 and became the leading Golf Analyst for that network for the next thirty-five years before retiring in 2002. Ken commented on his reign as a golf analyst, "I was the lead analyst for thirty-five years and that's the longest running lead analyst in the history of sports, not just golf, sports!" He received the John F. Kennedy Award for most memorable victory, inducted into the Collegiate Hall of Fame in 1978 and inducted the following year into the Smithsonian Institute. He was named one of Golf's Legendary Teachers by the PGA of America, San Jose State Tower Award, Metropolitan Golf Writers Gold Tee Award, Chicago District Gold Association Distinguished Service Award and Old Tom Morris Award in 1997.

In addition, Ken was the recipient of The Ambassador of Golf Award in 1998, PGA Lifetime Achievement Award in Journalism in 1999, captain of the victorious United States Presidents Cup in 2000, received an honorary doctorate from Tri-State University in 2002 and received the Bing Crosby Tournament Sponsor Award in 2003.

In addition, Ken was a golf course design and consultant to various corporate affiliations. As an announcer, Ken shared, "You can say more with a few words. Quoting Joe DiMaggio, 'When you're good you can always get in, it's knowing when to get out.' I feel I made the right decision and I credit that to Joe D. It was time to get out." Ken Venturi had been involved in many charitable interests, namely Guiding Eyes for the Blind, board member Loma Linda University School of Medicine Proton Beam Cancer Treatment, Kerry Mental Health (In Ireland) and the National Stuttering Foundation Spokesman. Mary Jane and I were proud and honored to call Ken and Kathleen Venturi our friends. We think of him often and miss his true friendship. He left us with rich and fond memories and left us too soon, in 2013 at the age of 82. Ken always said, "The world will not remember you for what you take from it, they'll only remember you for what you leave behind."

He left a lot behind, and it's a legacy to be proud of.

Clint Walker

Actor

Interviewed: 2003

I MET CLINT WALKER WHILE WE WERE BOTH under contract to Warner Bros. Studios in the late 1950s. One of my first jobs while under contract was an episode of *Cheyenne* starring Clint. He had a great presence, a handsome dude who stood 6-feet-6 inches tall, muscular, soft-spoken and a gentleman. He made the perfect Cheyenne Bodie.

The series ranked one of the best in the western genre for eight years. Clint shared with me, "I had no idea at all that I'd ever wind up in Hollywood and become a western star myself. I never had any serious thought about it. Seemed much too far out." He was a joy to work with, always on time, knew his dialogue, no temper tantrums, very honest and highly professional. I did four shows on *Cheyenne* and it was a pleasure to work with him.

Norman Eugene Walker was born in a small farm town in Illinois and did heavy physical work growing up, which lent to his imposing physique. Walker's Hollywood career began in Las Vegas of all places. "I moved to Las Vegas as a security guard in the casinos and a lot of celebrities would stop and talk to me. Lena Horn, Brian Dunlevy, Van Johnson, they all said, 'You oughta try show business. A big well-built guy like you, you might do alright.'" He continued, "An agent came in and gave me his card and said, 'Well, think it over and if you get interested, come to Hollywood and we'll see what we can do for you, but can't guarantee ya anything.'"

With the success of the *Cheyenne* series, he became a big star within a year. Clint said, "Jack Warner decided I was the guy to play Cheyenne. He gave me the name of Clint, which I liked. I think I had an edge because I was already under contract, but they got me much cheaper than they got the other guys."

He went on to appear in approximately thirty motion pictures including *Fort Dobbs*, which I appeared in, *Yellowstone Kelly*, *Gold of The Seven Saints*, *Sam Whiskey*, *More Dead Than Alive*, *None but the Brave*, *The Great Bank Robbery*, *The Dirty Dozen*, *Deadly Harvest*,

Clint Walker

![Signed photo: "Best wishes Michael and Mary Jane. Nice to see you again. Your friend, Clint Walker"]

Send Me No Flowers and his favorite, *Night of The Grizzly*. About *Grizzly*, "We had a wonderful cast and, which is really what makes a picture, and it was a good script and it turned out to be a wonderful little picture and they play it, play it, play it. But people love it."

None but the Brave, produced by Paramount Pictures, was helmed by first time director Frank Sinatra. Walker had some very nice things to say about Sinatra. "He was very nice to people and was far more talented than I ever realized. He had all of us over to his home one night for a spaghetti dinner. He entertained us for almost three hours, just telling jokes and funny stories and he was very good at it, too. If you really watched Frank, he was a very good actor, I felt honored to work with him. I learned, if he said he was your friend, he's your friend!"

Walker worked with some of the finest talents in show business such as Virginia Mayo, Ozzie Davis, Anne Francis, Kim Novak, Doris Day, Lee Marvin, Telly Savalas, Stephanie Powers, Edgar Buchanan, Yvette Mimieux, Charles Bronson, Burl Ives, Rock Hudson, Richard Basehart and many more.

Clint would tell his story from time to time, but not often, that he had a freak accident while skiing at Mammoth Mountain. It happened when a ski pole pierced his heart and almost cost him his life. "I asked God to let me come back, that's just the whole thing."

Another interesting fact about Clint that not all of his admirers knew, was that he had a terrific singing voice. He recorded an album of songs and ballads for Warner Bros. Records while under contract to the studio.

He also received a Golden Boot Award in 1997, considered the Oscar of westerns. Clint made many appearances at charity benefits and western film festivals. The lines to get his autograph were always the longest. Walker also wrote a 2003 western novel, entitled *Jockey Gold*.

I spoke with Clint two weeks before he passed away in May 2018, at the age of 90. I will always remember how knowledgeable he was about holistic medicine and how his mind was sharp and his memory was excellent. He was very humble and appreciative of his success.

Walker was a great American Patriot, and I am proud to have known him, to have worked with him and most of all, to have been his friend.

Clint's belief was, "I'm a very lucky guy. There is a God and he's there for you. You must have the faith and ask him."

Joseph Wambaugh
Writer
Interviewed: 2007

I MET MY NEIGHBOR, AWARD-WINNING NOVELIST, Joseph Wambaugh in 2007. I finished reading his latest book at the time, *Hollywood Station*, and it was an excellent read. I emailed Joseph and told him how much I enjoyed it, as well as his previous books, *The Choir Boys* and *The Onion Field*. I asked him if he would be my guest on my radio show and he graciously accepted. We set a date to do the show at his home. My wife, Mary Jane and I were warmly greeted by his wife Dee, as we set up our equipment and met Joseph for the first time. He was informative and highly professional during the entire interview. After that day, we kept in touch and Joseph was always friendly and very respectful. I know he enjoyed being a guest on my radio show.

At the time of my interview, Wambaugh had written eleven best-selling novels. *Hollywood Station* was a return to his Los Angeles Police Department roots. He portrayed how life was for cops in Los Angeles, and how it changed in 20 years. His best-selling novels include, *The New Centurions, The Blue Knight, The Choir Boys, The Black Marble, The Glitter Dome, The Delta Star, The Secrets of Harry Bright, The Golden Orange, Fugitive Nights, Finnegan's We,* and *Floaters*. Wambaugh revealed, "I think I really became a writer with the *Choir Boys*. That's when I could let it all go. "I had planned on perhaps writing, when I retired, but I just got started as a closet writer and one of the magazines, the *Atlantic Monthly*, suggested that I try a novel. Within three months, they had a novel, *The New Centurions*, sitting on their desk."

Wambaugh wrote five non-fiction books, *The Onion Field, Lines and Shadows, Echoes in The Darkness, The Blooding,* and *Fire Lover*.

He also wrote the screenplays for *The Onion Field* and *The Black Marble*. About *The Onion Field,* Joseph told us about the officer that survived. "Unfortunately, this was in the days preceding police departments being aware of delayed traumatic stress and he was

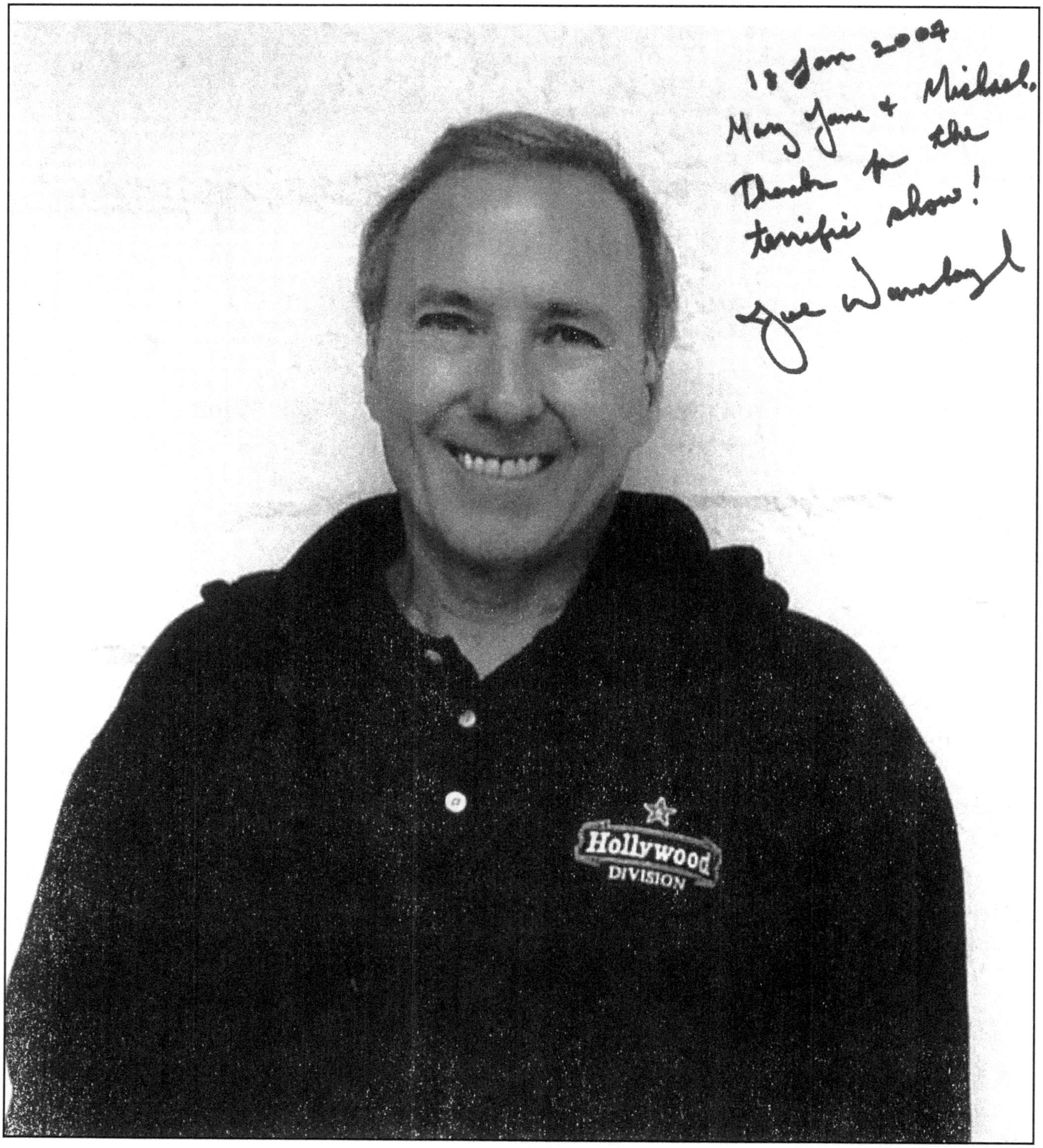
18 Jan 2004
Mary Jane & Michael,
Thanks for the
terrific show!
Hollywood
DIVISION

treated as though he should not have given up his gun, as though that act of his caused the death of his partner. Unconscious guilt, calling out for help. It was a frightening experience for me to write the book." He continued, "After *The Onion Field*, police departments all over the country became more aware of delayed traumatic stress."

He wrote the teleplays for the miniseries, *Echoes in The Darkness* and *Fugitive Nights*. He was the creator and consultant for the television series, *Police Story* and *The Blue Knight*. "I probably always felt good about cops because my dad had been one. That might have had some influence." *The New Centurions* and *Choir Boys* were adapted for the big screen. *The Blue Knights* was a television miniseries and a regular series for CBS. "I consulted on it, and the television series, as well." It was the first mini-series produced in America, actually." Eight of his books have become feature films, television movies or miniseries.

Joseph said, "When you're writing, it's like acting. You inhabit the character of the people you're writing about, kind of become those people, just as an actor becomes the character he's portraying. I guess, it was ten years of police work and what I learned about life and people and myself. It was just something I wanted to write down. I liked to read. I always had." With a humble smile he then added, "A working cop in Los Angeles produced this blockbuster book and film with George C. Scott. They were making movies and television shows from my stuff you know, and I'm supposed to be arresting someone and everyone I arrested wanted a part in a Wambaugh movie."

We learned that Wambaugh did have one regret. He always regretted not staying in the police force the full twenty years, leaving six years short of receiving his pension. There was something that wasn't finished in his life but there was no way he could have stayed on, with the amount of attention that was swirling around him at all times.

As an award-winning actor and author, I was very impressed by Joseph Wambaugh's literary talent and the suspenseful way he writes; allowing the reader to understand and thoroughly enjoy his stories in print, on television and on the big screen.

Dawn Wells
Actress
Interviewed: 2005

I MET ACTRESS DAWN WELLS when she arrived on the set of *Winterhawk* to portray the part of Clayanna Finley in September of 1975, I played the title role of the Blackfoot Chief, Winterhawk. In this story, Winterhawk and Clayanna fall in love and ride off into the sunset at the end of the film. Dawn did an outstanding job as well as handling the narration throughout the film with a sincere approach to the story and the characters.

Dawn was best known as the young darling, Mary Ann, in the highly successful television series, *Gilligan's Island*. Commenting on the show, Dawn shared, "On *Gilligan's Island*, how did we know we were funny? On film it's much harder to know than on stage. It was a family, we really loved each other." She added, "Two of the most successful shows in the history of television were *Gilligan's Island* and *The Brady Bunch*." Wells also appeared in more than 150 television shows, over 70 theatrical productions, and a number of feature films. Some of her television guest appearances included *Baywatch, Growing Pains, Matt Houston, Fantasy Island, The Love Boat, Vegas, The F.B.I, Bonanza, Wild Wild West, Laramie, Wells Fargo* and *Wagon Train*.

Some of Dawn's best-known feature films were *The New Interns, High Rollers, The Town That Dreaded Sundown, Return to Boggy Creek, High School U.S.A. Super Suckers* and, of course, *Winterhawk*.

Dawn also appeared in theatrical productions from Neil Simon to Tennessee Williams. She spent three months in Calgary starring in *The Tale of the Allergist Wife*, starred in *Love Letters* with Adam West in New Hampshire, Wyoming and Nevada, the musical *Nutcrackers* in Detroit, *Always Patsy Cline* in Florida and in the North American premier of Lawrence Roman's *Make Me a Match*.

"I love the stage," admitted Dawn. "I think what I love the most about the stage is the rehearsal part. In film, we don't get that chance very much. I love that opportunity of

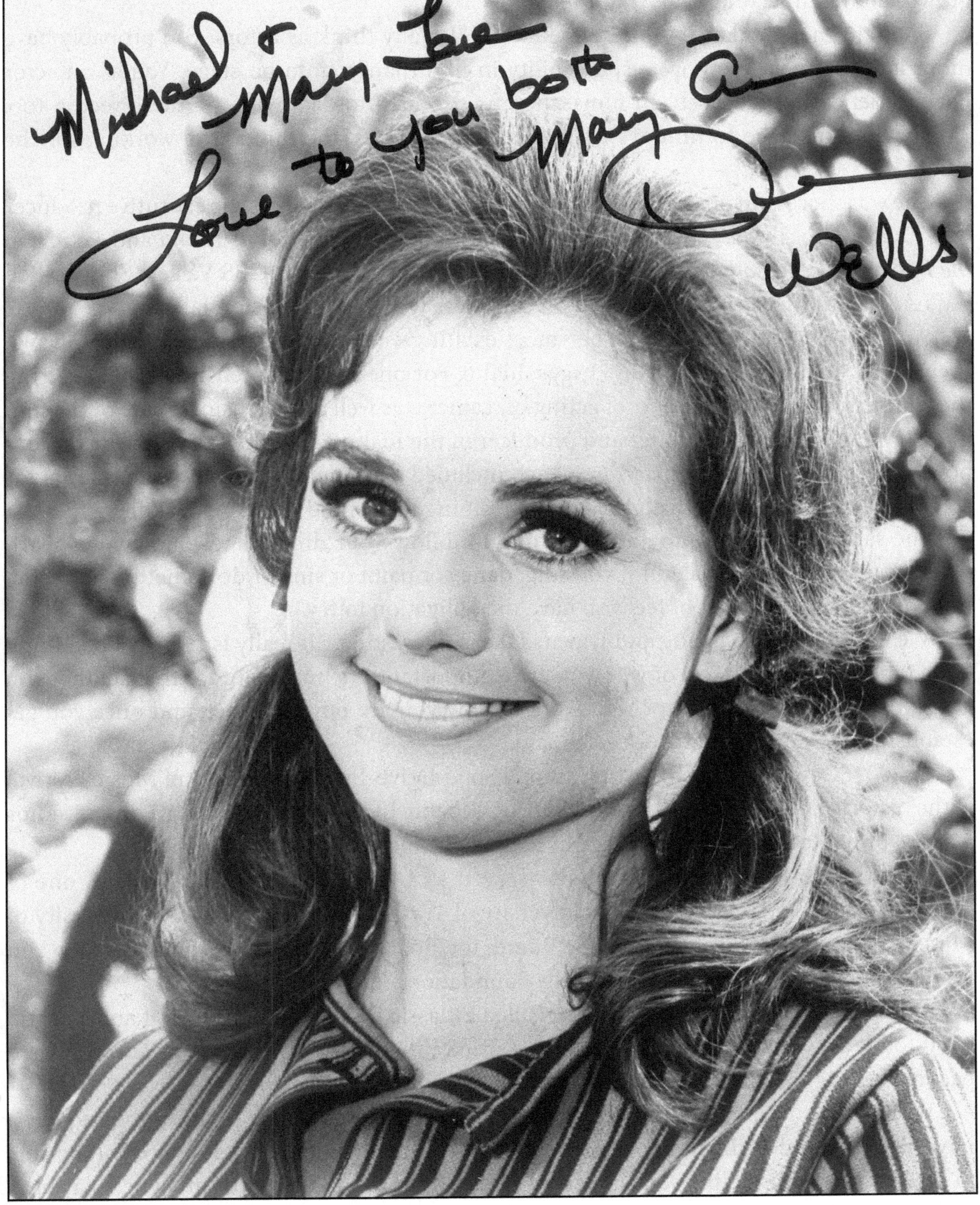
Michael &
Mary Love
Love to you both
Mary Ann
Wells

exploring the characters and trying things and working with it, all of that. It's a creative growth all the time and that's what I like."

She said there's nuance in these mediums: "I really think as actors, you probably have more independence or more responsibility in film than you do on stage. You as an actor have to depend on yourself. In films, there is so much to deal with, by the director, too. Comparing the stage to film, it's done in bits and pieces, the director is working for the whole."

She was successful on the other side of the camera, too. Dawn was the executive producer of *TV's Reel Adventures*, co-executive producer in *Surviving Gilligan's Island* and *Return to the Batcave: The Misadventures of Adam and Bert*. Dawn hosted a CBS Variety Show called *TV's All-Time Favorites* and appeared on countless radio and television talk shows.

At the time of this interview, her most exciting endeavor was establishing the Dawn Wells Film Actors Boot Camp, in Driggs, Idaho. For one week of intensive sessions during the summer, actors learn the art of acting on camera, as well as the business side of the film industry. Dawn was the founder and producer of the Idaho Film and Television Institute, a non-profit educational organization, which included a fast-track accredited film school for actors and crew members that gave college training for behind the camera skills.

She said, "We are training and teaching to follow your dream and follow your heart. And if God's given you that gift if you sing, dance or paint or sing or do something else that nobody else can do, I sort of feel you have the obligation to try."

We discussed typecasting and Dawn's take is interesting. "It really isn't such a bad thing to be typecast. The physical of who you are is important. It's important for the fact that you can get these jobs. As an actor, you work at how you are physically set, and once you get established, go do something else," she said.

In 2004, Dawn produced the first annual Spud Drive-In Family Film and Music Festival at the historic Spud Drive-In Theater in Driggs, Idaho. In addition, Wells' Tri-Power Studios was the only professional soundstage in Idaho, Wyoming or Montana.

As if that wasn't enough, Dawn also served as a trustee for Stephens College, one of her alma maters, and a graduate of University of Washington. She sat on the University of Missouri Children's Hospital Advisory Board, the Board of Women in Film and Video and was also chairman of the Terry Lee Wells Foundation.

The 1975 film *Winterhawk* has been called a classic by all who have seen it and can still see it today on various streaming platforms. Today, there are only three of us left who were part of the original ensemble cast in the film.

I wanted to keep the character of Winterhawk alive and have written the sequel, a novella, *Winterhawk's Land*. It has garnered five-star reviews and hopefully we will be able to see this story on the big screen. It continues twenty years later with my wife, Clayanna and our son. Hopefully in the not too-distant future, I look forward to filming *Winterhawk's*

Land. Dawn and I were perfectly cast in the original film but sadly, she passed away in 2020 at the age of 82. Unfortunately we are not able to reprise our roles together but knowing her so well, I'm sure she would agree that's it's a story that still needs to be told. I agreed with Dawn when she said, "I believe that everything is possible. I'm a real optimist."

Dawn Wells proved that time and time again.

Jerry West
Basketball – Hall of Fame
Interviewed: 1995

My interview with Jerry West took place at the Café Roma Restaurant in Beverly Hills, California. The first time I met Jerry West was at Café Roma. There were quite a few other entertainers, actors, directors and producers that attended from time to time. Jerry walked in one afternoon looking around the room, seemingly looking for someone he was to meet there. A couple of guys knew him and waved him over to our table. He took a few strides to our table when Norm Crosby invited him to sit and have lunch with us, but not before he introduced Jerry to everyone. We were all big fans of his and the Los Angeles Lakers. He was very receptive and enjoyed a quick joke told by Shecky Greene. Before he left to join his friends for lunch, I told him that Gary Vitti, the trainer for the Lakers, was my cousin. He was delighted to hear that; he liked and respected Gary very much.

Jerry was born in the town of Chelyan, West Virginia. Jerry smiled, "Michael, I wouldn't exactly call this a town, it's about 500 people. I lived in a very small, little place. It was tough growing up. I grew up to be somewhat of a loner. Your best friend is your mind and I know growing up, obviously that was important for me."

He first garnered national attention as a high school basketball star in his senior year, by leading East Bank High School to the state title and became the first prep player in the state's history to register over 900 points in a single season. West went on to become a two-time All American at the University of West Virginia and finished his collegiate basketball career with a 24.8 scoring average. He was drafted by the Los Angeles Lakers in the first round of the 1960 college draft.

After he joined the Lakers, Mr. Clutch established himself as one of the greatest players in NBA history throughout his brilliant fourteen-year career with the team. I asked Jerry who gave him the wonderful descriptive, 'Mr. Clutch.' Smiling, he said, "Well, obviously it

was Chick Hearn." Chick was the long time announcer for the Los Angeles Lakers. "He seems to find some nickname or some attribute of a player that he will apply nicknames to."

Jerry led the team in scoring, seven of those fourteen years averaging 30 plus points, four times. He is the Lakers all-time scoring leader and the 22nd leading scorer in NBA history (25,192) points. Jerry shared, "I'd rather take a risk, than not take a risk. And it became easier as my career went on. I felt incredible confidence that I could do something when the game mattered."

When he retired following the 1973–74 season, he had become only the third player to surpass the 25,000 points plateaus, finishing with a career scoring average of 27 points per game, which ranked him the fourth best in NBA history. "The one thing athletes have to have; you have to have courage. Those are lessons I learned at a very early age. If you wanted something you worked as hard as you could to get it but you didn't give up. I was blessed with quickness and jumping ability."

His 29.1 playoff scoring average is second only to Michael Jordan. West was selected to the All-NBA first team ten times and in the NBA's All-Defensive first team, four times. He was inducted into the National Basketball Association Hall of Fame in 1979. Jerry was named to the NBA's 35th Anniversary Team in 1980.

After retiring before the 1974–75 season, he returned to the Lakers as the club's head coach for three years, compiling 145 wins against 101 losses. Following his coaching, Jerry spent three years as a special consultant with the Lakers before becoming General Manager. For twelve years, he successfully handled the day-to-day operations in all player personnel decisions and what an outstanding job he did!

Nobody has had more success as a player and an executive than Mr. Clutch. He had fourteen All-Star appearances in fourteen seasons as a player, received NBA Executive of the Year Awards as a member of the front office, while he was still playing, and three as General Manager. West laid the foundation for other ex-players to become executives, before leaving the Los Angeles Lakers in 2002. Jerry had this to say about his legendary career, "Most of the time, you could almost write it. My scoring would be; it was gonna be from 25 to 40 points every night. That's the thing I'm most proud of in my career."

Jerry is the proud father of his own basketball team of five sons. He and his wife Karen are the parents of their sons, Ryan and Jonathan. He has three sons David, Mark and Michael from a previous marriage.

The tag Mr. Clutch is most fitting for Jerry West, on and off the court.

Jonathan Winters
Entertainer
Interviewed: 2003

I MET JONATHAN WINTERS AT A CELEBRITY charity tennis tournament many years ago. He was my doubles partner in one of the matches. We didn't do very well against our opponents, but we had a lot of laughs. It was the beginning of a long friendship I had with one of the greatest comedians of all time.

Jonathan owned a beautiful house near the Toluca Lake Golf Course and a stone's throw from the Warner Bros. Studios in Burbank, California. Our relationship continued with an invitation by Jonathan and his wife Eileen, who liked to have their friends come to their home for tennis matches and lunch. I was very pleased to be invited on several occasions and always had a fun afternoon of tennis, a nice luncheon afterwards, surrounded by contagious laughter.

Jonathan heard that I was a former professional baseball player before I became an actor. He was born and raised in Dayton, Ohio and told me that he had been a big Cincinnati Reds baseball fan since he was a boy, and how much he loved baseball. I asked Jonathan and Eileen if they would like to attend a Dodger game when the Cincinnati Reds came to town. Jonathan said he would love to go. A couple of weeks later, Cincinnati visited Dodger Stadium for a three-game series and I invited Jonathan to come with me and he immediately accepted. I knew Dodger manager Tommy Lasorda, and Al Campanis, general manager in charge of player personnel, as well as some of the Dodgers and Cincinnati ballplayers. I made a phone call when they got to town and we were invited to the Cincinnati clubhouse before the game.

I introduced Jonathan to everyone, including Reds manager Sparky Anderson. All the players circled around him and he began to go into character and improvise a very heated discussion between two players, who were both playing their boombox radios much too loud, at the same time. He was so hysterical, they were crying with laughter, falling to their

knees from laughing so hard. Jonathan did twenty minutes of the most brilliant and perfect imitations of these two disgruntled characters, something that none of them had ever seen or heard before.

His improvisation was spot-on. I'm sure Sparky and the ballplayers never forgot it for the rest of their lives. Time was running out and the guys had to get ready for the game. We were invited back any time they were in town. We went to our seats and watched Cincinnati beat the Dodgers 5-4.

Growing up, Jonathan shared, "I was brought up to address everybody, regardless of color, man or a woman, you called them Miss, Mrs. or Mr., until they told you otherwise. My grandfather was my number one role model."

Winters started his entertainment career in radio. During our interview he described radio as, "A world of imagination." He made people laugh in all of his motion pictures, television and variety shows, throughout the years. He brought a new kind of comedy to American television and films with his improvisatorial brilliance. He created such memorable characters as Maude Fricket. "Maude Fricket was modeled after my Aunt and she was not short of marbles at all!" Chester Honeyhugger and Elwood P. Suggins were also his incredibly funny character creations. "A lot of my characters you have to wait a little, for development."

Winters appeared on all the top variety shows such as *The Jack Parr Show*, which Jonathan commented, "For Jack Parr, you had to produce."

His other TV performances included, *The Gary Moore Show, The Arthur Godfrey Show, The Andy William Show, The Bob Hope Show, The Carol Burnett Show, Rowan and Martin's Laugh In, The Tonight Show starring Johnny Carson, The David Lettermen Show*, including hosting his own show, *The Jonathan Winters Show* and *The Wacky World of Jonathan Winters*.

He became a regular ABC's *Mork and Mindy*. He recalled, "The first day on *Mork and Mindy*, the first thing Robin Williams said to me was, 'you're my mentor.' Jonathan went on to win an Emmy Award for Best Supporting Actor in the show's segment. He also appeared in numerous motion pictures including, *The Loved One, Viva Max, Penelope, The Fish That Saved Pittsburgh, The Flintstones, The Adventures of Rocky and Bullwinkle, The Russians Are Coming the Russians Are Coming, It's a Mad, Mad, Mad, Mad World* and the list goes on.

When I interviewed Jonathan at his home in Montecito, California, he asked me if we could record the show in his guest house on the property. Jonathan knew it was a perfect location to give himself the space he needed to improvise. I hardly had to ask him any questions because I didn't want to disturb his brilliant roll. His ability to go into many characters instantly was second to none.

It was not an interview; it was a performance that flowed with each character he brought to life. Despite knowing him so well, I was still in awe of how each characterization was so different from the other. I truly wished I had a camera on him the whole time instead of just a microphone.

    I feel blessed to have been able to spend quality time with Jonathan Winters during our radio interview and to have been his friend with the privilege of enjoying his one-of-a-kind comedy entertainment, for so many years. He passed on, to entertain the heavens at age 87 in 2013.

Celebrity Radio Talk Show Host
Award Winning Actor/Award Winning Author
Michael Dante

www.michaeldanteway.com

Visit Michael Dante's website to learn more about the radio shows, watch special interviews with Michael, and catch up on our exclusive events!

"I know, I just know you're gonna to love it!"
Thank you, Michael Dante

www.ingramcontent.com/pod-product-compliance
Lightning Source LLC
Chambersburg PA
CBHW062129160426
43191CB00013B/2241